Praise

If you're looking for a management and team building book written by a business school professor who believes he/she knows all about the business world and how it works because he/she has taught for many years, then this book is not for you.

However, if you want to walk alongside someone who has lived a full life in corporate America and who has experienced and learned from the good and the not-so-good, then sit back and enjoy as Jed takes you through his experiences with insightful anecdotes.

You will find many useful "Takeaways," like how placing others first will lead to success for both the individual and the team. Embedded in Jed's interesting stories and experiences are many important and practical lessons that, if applied, will make you a better employee or manager - guaranteed!

Lt. Colonel D. Michael Lucas, USAF (Retired)

Jed Selter and I go back years in life and business. His ability to grasp the full essence of purpose, passion, and the true ingredients of what creates a meaningful life is commendable, as he has written in this book. Read it yourself, and share it with your children and, in my case, my grandchildren. Thank you for your gifts, brother Jed.

Dennis Broughton, President, Mountain Music Productions

Mr. Selter and I have collaborated on reading projects for children for the past two years and continue to do so.

"Please Pass the Potatoes" is a book worth reading. My takeaway through so much of the book was Mr. Selter's love for people, and how he created opportunities for others.

Mr. Selter recounts some painful experiences in the book, but I believe we have a duty to share our stories, as he has, to hopefully help someone else. I cringed at the description he shared when he thought the world would be better off without him. Again, someone probably needs to hear that.

In recounting the ins and outs of his management career, Mr. Selter conveys the importance of respecting others. Throughout his story, he provides practical tools and principles for how to manage ourselves and connect with people.

All in all, this book will challenge and inspire.

Kathryn Stansel, 4th Grade Reading Teacher

I thoroughly enjoyed Jed's recounting of his unique journey in business. He effectively weaves practical relationship principles into his story. Years ago, I had the opportunity to attend one of Jed's workshops and used this material throughout my 47-year management career in the Washington State Patrol and as the Kitsap County Sheriff. "Please Pass the Potatoes" is a very worthwhile and useful read.

Steve Boyer, Kitsap County Sheriff (Retired)

From his many, varied, and even dramatic experiences, Jed Selter has chosen the most important life lessons to recount in this book. His wise and provocative reflections and questions prompt us all to be more fearless, authentic, and generous.

Dr. Noelle Sterne, Author, Editor

Successful businesses—as well as most human endeavors—depend on strong relationships. In this memoir, reflecting on his colorful career, Jed Selter speaks to the interpersonal behaviors and principles foundational to cementing exceptional relationships. Readers will benefit personally and professionally from the author's advice and considerations for relationship building employing his "we" versus "me" centered approach.

Gaston Peter-Contesse, Chief Financial Officer (Retired)

Please Pass the Potatoes

Please Pass The Potatoes
A Memoir—Nourishing Exceptional Relationships
First edition, published 2024

Written by Jed Selter
Copyright © 2024 by Jed Selter
All Rights Reserved

Softcover ISBN 978-1-952685-82-8

No part of this book may be reproduced, stored in or introduced into a retrieval system, or transmitted, in any form or by any means (electronic, mechanical, photocopying, recording, or otherwise) without the prior written permission of the author.

Published by Kitsap Publishing
Poulsbo, 98370 WA
www.KitsapPublishing.com

A Memoir

PLEASE PASS THE POTATOES

Nourishing Exceptional Relationships

by Jed Selter

With Appreciation

I sincerely want to thank several people who have reviewed and made this book so much better than my initial offering. They include my wife, Darla; my sister, Noelle; and my good friend, Gaston. Each of them took a fresh look at my writing and gave me exceptional input to improve the book.

Special recognition goes to one more person—Mike Lucas.

Mike and I joined the Air Force Office of Special Investigations (AFOSI) as brand new 2nd Lieutenants and bachelors. We roomed together in a couple of locations in the Washington, D.C. area and had some great fun times—none of which either of us will ever acknowledge publicly. But then, our paths in AFOSI went in different directions. We lost contact for several years when I left the Air Force. Mike completed a 23-year career in the Air Force and retired as a Lieutenant Colonel.

We connected again for several years after I had been with my last company on the West Coast. Mike was hired as an investigator and then became the investigative manager for the company. We stayed connected and thoroughly enjoyed each other until I retired in 2000, and then, again, we lost touch.

Mike recently contacted me and we struck up our previous wonderful relationship like we never missed a beat. We were once again like two little excited kids in a candy store, laughing and giggling together at almost everything. Mike has always challenged me and made me laugh like no one else I have ever known. Nothing has changed.

As I started on this book's second draft, I asked Mike if he would consider reviewing it. He has done so much more than I would have ever expected or asked for. Mike challenged me in many parts of the book, asked incisive questions, and encouraged me to provide more detail. His thoughts and insightful comments have significantly improved the clarity and tone of what you will read.

Mike—as with Darla, Noelle, and Gaston—I cannot thank you enough!

From the Publisher

The title *"Please Pass the Potatoes"* is deeply symbolic and ties directly to the core message of Jed Selter's memoir, which is about the importance of selflessness, generosity, and placing others' needs before one's own in both personal and professional contexts. The act of passing the potatoes at a dinner table, a seemingly simple gesture of courtesy and awareness of others' needs, becomes a powerful metaphor for the kind of leadership and relationship management Selter advocates for throughout the book.

This title encapsulates the essence of the memoir's unique approach to discussing leadership and management—not through the lens of dominating or outmaneuvering others, but through the act of service, consideration, and building meaningful connections. It signifies the value of contributing to the well-being of the team and the organization by ensuring that others' needs are met before one's own. This approach fosters an environment of trust, mutual respect, and collaboration, which, as Selter's anecdotes and experiences demonstrate, are crucial for creating successful and sustainable relationships and organizational cultures.

By choosing this title, Selter invites readers to reflect on the impact that everyday acts of kindness and consideration can have on their professional environments and personal lives. It encourages a shift from a "me-first" to a "we-first" mentality, highlighting that the true measure of success, both as individuals and leaders, lies in how we support and uplift those around us. *"Please Pass the Potatoes"* thus becomes more than just a book on management; it's a call to embrace a more compassionate and service-oriented approach to leadership and life.

On behalf of Kitsap Publishing, I am proud to present *"Please Pass the Potatoes"* by Jed Selter. May this book serve as a guidepost for those seeking to forge deeper connections, build stronger teams, and lead with a renewed sense of purpose and humanity.

Ingemar Anderson

Preface

Picture yourself at a lavish holiday dinner—candles flickering on a gorgeously set table, quiet music in the background, a festive centerpiece, a golden brown roast turkey in the middle, all the trimmings, and that beautifully laid out bowl of wonderful high carb mashed potatoes topped with generous pads of dripping yummy butter.

And, like everyone else eyeing those potatoes—prepared with great love and ready for the taking—you are dying to get your share! Those potatoes are calling you!

Of course, you could lunge across the table, grab them, and give yourself a pound full helping, ignoring the rest of the group. But where would that get you? Probably a lot of frowns, maybe a few growls, and certainly a stomachache.

Nope, be considerate. Put others first. Pass that bowl around the table first, insisting on taking a spoonful or two only after everyone else has had theirs. What have you got to lose? A few potatoes?

So what if the bowl is almost empty when it comes to you? For your sacrifice, you have helped everyone else get what they want. People will appreciate you for thinking of them. And it's likely that you won't remember those potatoes in the morning. If you do, you'll be glad you didn't have the extra calories.

But there is more. Although it is not your intent, your action will benefit you in a profound and humbling way. Accepting gratitude from others will bring you a quiet and peaceful joy. This may sound corny, but it is not an overstatement. (When you next find yourself in a position to put others first, try it. You will see these results for yourself.)

The story of "passing the potatoes" is an apt description for relationships in life.

We can consciously choose how we want to relate to others.

In working together, if I decide to include what you want or need, not just what I want, we can develop a respectful and trusting relationship. This is the essence of successful collaboration. It will help ensure that working together will accomplish effective results.

This book is my personal story. But it is more than a memoir or the typical "how to" management and relationship book.

Woven through my experiences are proven relationship and attitudinal principles that lead to success with others. I discovered and learned to use these principles during my nearly forty years in the U.S. Air Force and corporate America.

Over the years, I have been fortunate to work with thousands of business professionals at every level as well as students in elementary, high school and college environments. I have seen the unquestionable positive results from their increased awareness as they have used the principles in this book.

When you too use the material here, you can significantly improve your relationships.

For illustrative purposes, I have changed some descriptive elements of my story, speaking in general terms of some situations and organizations to protect sensitive information and circumstances. But the basics of the story are true.

Several chapters conclude with "Takeaways" and related "Introspections." These are lessons learned and helpful exercises from my experiences described in these chapters.

You will note that I have repeated the book's title in a few places. This is my shorthand for emphasizing the principles discussed for establishing positive relationships.

Jed Selter

Attitude

The longer I live, the more I realize the impact of attitude on my life. Attitude is more important than facts. It is more important than the past, than education, than money, than circumstances, than failures, than successes, than what other people think or say or do. It is more important than appearance, or giftedness, or skill. It will make or break a company . . . a church . . . a home . . . a person.

The remarkable thing is we have a choice every day regarding the attitude we will embrace for that day. We cannot change our past…we cannot change the fact that people will act in a certain way. We cannot change the inevitable . . . the only thing we can do is play the one string we have, and that is our attitude.

I am convinced that life is ten percent what happens to me and ninety percent how I react to it. And so it is with you . . . .

You are in charge of your attitude.

Charles R. Swindoll

Contents

Praise	
With Appreciation	I
From the Publisher	III
Preface	V
Attitude	VIII
Chapter 1: Looking Back	1
Takeaway: Understand Fear, But Do Not Be Fearful	3
Introspection: About Fear	4
Chapter 2: The Beginning	7
Chapter 3: First Big Break	10
Chapter 4: Transition	16
Chapter 5: A Way to Relate	20
Takeaway: A Way to Relate	22
Introspection: A Way to Relate	23
Chapter 6: The Next Big Move	24
Chapter 7: Back to Basics	27
Chapter 8: Expanded Responsibilities	30
Chapter 9: Unusual Assignments	33
Chapter 10: Leading National Action	38
Chapter 11: More Significant Assignments	45
Chapter 12: Competition and Winning and Losing	48
Takeaway: Winning and Losing	51
Introspection: Winning and Losing	52
Takeaway: Destructive Extreme Competitiveness	53
Introspection: Destructive Competitiveness	54
Chapter 13: The Balloon Bursts	56
Chapter 14: Fall Into Depression	60
Chapter 15: Safe Landing	67
Chapter 16: New Beginning	72
Takeaway: Focus for Common Purpose	74
Introspection: Focus for Common Purpose	75
Chapter 17: Audits	77
Chapter 18: Tough Decision	80
Chapter 19: Another Transition	85

Chapter 20: Last Company Project   90
Chapter 21: Moving Forward   100
   Takeaway: "We First" Instead of "Me First"   104
   Introspection: "Me First" or "We First"   105
Chapter 22: Beyond Business   106
Chapter 23: Caring Clowns International (CCI)   109
Chapter 24: Conclusion   118
More About the Author   122

1

Looking Back

Looking back on my career, I had a good run. Like most folks who have been working for many years, I had some ups and downs, but overall, I was successful, and for the most part, I enjoyed what I did.

My few downsides were significant, but they always set me up to reflect and learn. Even though they created some anxiety, uncertainty, and pain, they helped me become a more effective manager and moved my career forward.

A key for me was to make opportunities for myself to take on new challenges and excel as much as I could. In many cases, this involved taking risks—and the fear of failure. Fear was an emotion that I had to overcome several times in my business journey.

Sometimes this was a scary proposition, and I had to beat down those voices in my head telling me I couldn't do what I committed to. I admit I was very frightened that I might fail.

But early in my career, I realized fear was an unwelcome component of performing new jobs. I intentionally walked into situations knowing that I lacked experience. But even though I had confidence in my abilities, there was always a certain niggling at the back of my mind—a wondering whether I could meet the challenges of these jobs.

I had to concede, at least to myself, that I feared I might not succeed. I knew I had to manage and conquer this fear before I could move forward with confidence. Over time, I learned how to do that.

Fear is a complicated emotion. One that we need to understand.

In many situations, fear of something can be a life saver. It can be healthy, like fear of falling. It can heighten your sensitivities, so you are more acutely aware of dangers and help you instinctively react to stay out of harm's way.

But in business, in relationships, fear can be an insidious and unconscious detriment. It can cause you to lash out at others or conversely to withdraw or become protective of yourself. In any case, it can blur your perceptions, and negatively affect your ability to make good decisions.

Being afraid in the business setting is self-destructive. It increases anxiety and inhibits your observing, listening, and thinking clearly. It dulls your senses. It paralyzes. It can rob you of the ability to act.

That's not all. Fear can ruin trust in relationships and can cause disconnects with others. It can create suspicion and isolation.

In combating and learning how to manage fear, it is useful to look at the underlying reasons for it and to analyze how to manage and dissipate it.

There are important questions to ask yourself to get at the root of your fear. What are the reasons underlying your fear and what can you do to address them? What is in your control to change the circumstances that are creating the fear?

Takeaway

Understand Fear, But Do Not Be Fearful

- In relationships, being fearful is self-destructive.
- Fear will increase anxiety and dull one's senses. It inhibits hearing, listening, and thinking clearly.
- Fear ruins trust in relationships and causes disconnects with others. It can create suspicion and isolation.
- Fear paralyzes and will rob you of the ability to act.
- Fear must be recognized and worked through as quickly as possible so you can function to your fullest capabilities, staying connected with others in mutually supportive and respectful relationships.

Introspection

About Fear

This exercise is intended to help you become aware of and deal with fear.

- Think about something you are afraid of and write it down. (It can be anything: a situation, a responsibility, a relationship in your personal or professional life, or fear of rejection or failure.)

- How does this fear manifest itself in you? It is essential to identify and recognize how this fear affects you. Write down how this fear affects you (such as feeling confused, feeling angry, being agitated, sweating, muscle tenseness, headaches, or lack of self-confidence).

- List some reasons for this fear (such as insecurity or newness in a relationship, or lack of experience to deal with a situation).

- For each of the reasons above, describe reasonable actions you can take to change the course of the fear (such as opening to a new relationship or reflecting on previous experiences that may relate to a new challenge).

- Test each action by taking that action and observing if it lessens the effects of the fear you described above.

- To ensure success, you may need to repeat the steps. Use this process to tackle other fears you may have.

- If this process is not successful, list new reasons and actions. Follow your progress, ensuring that you are honest and truthful with yourself about the reasons and actions you describe and use.

<u>Expected Outcome:</u> Gain an understanding of fear in your life and how to analyze it to dissipate its effect.

I had my bouts getting caught in the middle of the political moves of others, but I was able to weather those storms and come out on the sunny side.

Early on, I learned to listen to my inner self and understand what motivated me. This self-talk is a must to grow.

I realized that the only thing I can control is my attitude and how I react to whatever is in front of me. This includes how I interact with others.

Time and time again, I saw that if I managed my attitude—being open, respectful, and sincerely listening to hear what people were saying, not just waiting when they spoke to weigh in with my own two cents, I could have excellent relationships with other people.

And I could use this consciousness to deal with my bosses, peers, those in the organizations I managed, and others with whom I did business.

As a point of reference and mindset, in managing organizations, I have never talked about "people who worked for me." In truth, with the proper positive reinforcement, everybody works for themselves.

I always saw my job as someone to open doors and empower others, to provide people opportunities to think for themselves and be proud of the things they could accomplish.

That is not to say that some people did not become problems. Although just a few, some were. But even then, there was a way to counsel them and respectfully address things that needed improvement.

Please pass the potatoes.

2

The Beginning

When I graduated from college, I was commissioned as an officer in the U.S. Air Force. My designation as a Distinguished Military Graduate gave me some notoriety. It wasn't until later in my brief military career that I would see how this set me up for a plum assignment in the Pentagon and my future in business. More on that later.

I was given the Distinguished Military Graduate designation because of my role as the Cadet Commander of the Air Force ROTC Student Corps in my senior year. I was at the top of the cadet pyramid, managing the Corps of about 350 ROTC students and reporting to an Air Force full colonel responsible for the ROTC Detachment. I was offered this position as a junior, but because my academic plate was full that year, I requested to be considered in my senior year.

This job was my first significant experience of stepping out of my comfort zone and taking on something entirely new. I had no idea what I was getting into, but I knew it was a potential opportunity to increase the options for my future.

To make things even more interesting, when I accepted the job, the colonel told me privately that this year's Corps of Cadets was made up of more mediocre students than in previous years, so my job would be more challenging to recruit an effective staff to help me manage the Cadet Corps and its business.

Nevertheless, I willingly jumped into the deep end with both feet.

The payoff for taking this assignment was that when I graduated and received my commission as an Air Force 2nd Lieutenant, I was offered my choice of organizational assignments in the Air Force, my choice of location, and a guaranteed 30-year "regular" commission as

an officer. At that time, regular commissions were primarily held for Air Force Academy graduates.

Most who graduated through the ROTC college program were offered 20-year "reserve" commissions renewable every five years at the Air Force's discretion.

These three benefits were significant rewards and would also expand my options in the Air Force and beyond.

When I graduated, I selected my Air Force assignment in Washington, D.C., at Air Force Headquarters in specialized investigative work in the Air Force Office of Special Investigations (AFOSI). It included all types of investigations for the Air Force, from personnel investigations for clearances, to criminal cases to counterespionage investigations.

Although each of us in the office held a regular Air Force rank, since the organization had been fashioned after the FBI, we were all designated as "Special Agents," carried special credentials and badges similar to FBI Special Agents and wore civilian suits instead of our military uniforms. This was heady stuff for a young 22-year-old new junior officer. And I was excited!

The point here is that each of us should take every opportunity to set our own path. While there may be risk and a small degree of fear involved, for the most part, accepting something new can lead to bigger and better things. And viewed in the proper light, it can be very rewarding!

My initial training was in counterespionage. Washington, D.C. was a ripe environment to work in this area with so many diplomatic operatives. The work was interesting but not much to my liking.

In suburban Maryland, where I relocated, I had started a Boy Scout Troop with another agent. Teaching young men ethics and good morals clashed seriously with my day job in the counterespionage world dealing with the black art of deceiving and manipulating people.

3

First Big Break

Even though I constantly felt the conflict between my job and scouting activities, I continued doing both. I knew something had to change, but I had no idea how or what would happen.

Then, out of the blue, one morning, our Deputy Director, a full colonel, called me into his office. I had never been in his office before or met him, although I knew who he was.

He said, "Jed, there is an assignment for you in the Pentagon on loan from our office. You have an interview this afternoon at 3 p.m."

I was taken aback. He knew my nickname. What? (My legal first name is Robert.) I was a brand-new 2nd Lieutenant with six months under my belt as an officer in the U.S. Air Force! What was going on?

I said as calmly as I could, "Yes, Sir. I will be there and thank you." He handed me a handwritten note with the office address in the Pentagon, and I left his office, stunned.

What could this be? Why me? Was I up for something new? Did I have the skills to be successful? What if I couldn't do the job? What would those who recommended me think of me then? The anxious foreboding of fear came over me but I managed to get beyond it and move forward. (I said to myself that if I did not have the potential to do this job, I would not have been selected for it. That quelled the momentary anxiety I was experiencing.) The possibility of another opportunity was scary but could be fantastic! Even though this was an unknown, which caused me some trepidation, it was exciting.

I had never been to the Pentagon. I took a cab to the Concourse entrance. It was a city in itself with a bus tunnel, shops, and eateries on the public concourse. People of all ranks and military services were bustling everywhere at a fast pace.

I walked up to an armed guard at the entrance to the interior of the building and said, "Excuse me." Looking down at the handwritten note, I said, "Can you direct me to office 1610, the fourth floor on the C Ring?" I handed the note to the guard.

The guard looked at the note and then at me. He said, "Sir, may I see your military ID, please?"

I pulled out my ID card, and the guard took out a map and showed me where the office was and how to get there.

If you have never been in the Pentagon, it can be overwhelming. It is a maze of corridors on each floor. It takes a map to find anything. You could wander for days and never get to where you needed to go.

With the help of the map the guard gave me I found the office and walked in to a small anteroom where two secretaries met me.

The anteroom was bordered by three large blue metal vault doors with built-in dials, not unlike what you might see in a small-town bank.

I was greeted casually by one of the secretaries. "Hi, Jed. They are waiting for you in Vault A behind you." More shock - like they already knew me.

"Just knock on the door," she said. And in a whisper, she smiled and added, "And don't worry, just relax."

Tentatively, I knocked on the vault door. A full colonel opened it. He extended his hand, casually introduced himself, and ushered me in, closing the vault door behind us.

The vault was spacious but drab. It was built to government standards to store securely and use highly sensitive compartmented Top Secret code-word material. In government parlance, this type of secure area is called a Sensitive Compartmented Information Facility (SCIF).

It was like a movie set. The windows were boarded up with opaque plates. Sound-deadening tiles covered the walls and ceiling. The walls, ceiling, and windows were fitted with steel mesh material to prevent emanations of electronic signals and electronic surveillance from outside the area. The single door and vault interior were fitted with motion detection and perimeter alarms, which were monitored after business hours when the vault was closed.

There were no pictures or other decorations on the walls. The bringing of electronic equipment into the SCIF was prohibited, and it was swept monthly for electronic eavesdropping devices. This was a secure facility!

Communications gear labeled "Top Secret" and a red secure phone sat in one corner. The rest of the walls were lined with gun metal gray heavy steel file cabinets, each with a built-in dial. The front of each cabinet had a large bold red sign reading "Top Secret."

In front of the filing cabinets toward the center of the room sat five high-ranking Air Force officers in uniform at their own desks. From the rows of military ribbons on their chests, it was apparent that they had years of experience in the Air Force. Four of them had senior pilot wings. (I was uncomfortably aware of my one measly ribbon: the combat ribbon everyone had because of the country's involvement in the Vietnam War.)

Each officer's desk was the typical cheap government-issue dull green metal. None of the desks displayed anything personal—no family photos or other personal items. Everything underscored the fact that the vault was a no-frills, stark working environment, only for "serious business."

This experience was definitely outside my comfort zone.

I stood in the middle of the room, dumbstruck and not knowing what to do. Should I salute, introduce myself, attempt to shake hands, or just stand and wait?

Before I could move, a colonel sitting at his desk greeted me softly—again by my nickname. "You can sit down and relax at the spare desk over there, Jed." He pointed to the only empty desk in the room.

The others in the room started with small talk to put me at ease. Then one of them abruptly said, "So, Jed, would you like to join us?"

I replied, "Thank you, Sir. Can you tell me anything about the job?"

He said, "Well, you will coordinate with a lot of folks in various offices and departments and with contractors, and the job will involve some travel. It will be exciting, but I can't tell you anything more until you accept the assignment and sign some security papers." He held up a small raft of papers with red-bordered "Top Secret/Sensitive Compartmented Information (SCI)" cover sheets.

After a brief moment, while they waited for my response, another colonel broke the awkward silence and said, "The job is yours if you want it. Think about it overnight, and either report at eight tomorrow morning or call, and we will find someone else, although we would prefer that you join us."

I stood up from the desk, thanked them, shook hands, and left the vault.

As I stepped into the main hallway, I said to myself, still remembering my exact words, "Why didn't they ask anything about me? Did they know everything? Did you see the rank in that room? What are you doing? How bad could this be?"

I immediately turned around, knocked on the vault door again, walked in, and said," Gentlemen, I would be honored to join you."

That spare desk was for me.

I held a position three levels above my current rank. This assignment was high-stakes and highly classified.

I was responsible for several support activities for our operations. It involved continuous liaison with components across the military services and federal agencies in the intelligence community and contractors, and daily briefings of generals and admirals who had been investigated and approved for access to what we were doing.

This job was a prestigious position for a new junior officer. At the time, there were probably only a few hundred of us across the military doing the type of support work I was involved in. It was rarified air.

After about two months on the job, it dawned on me that my having been the ROTC Cadet Commander and being designated as a Distinguished Military Graduate in college had unofficially labeled me as an "up and comer" as a young officer and was what gave me this job opportunity.

I was in this position for almost five years. I loved the job but knew I would eventually be reassigned to another function. So, toward the end of that assignment, I resigned my commission to go into industry, wanting to stay in the same type of work.

As an anecdote, the colonel who was the deputy for our small organization was one of the several senior pilots in the office. Years later, after he had passed away at the age of 99, I researched his background.

He started his Air Force career as a "Hump Pilot" in the Army Air Corp, which became the U.S. Air Force.

During World War II, the Hump Pilots and their crews served in the China-Berma-India Theater (CBI), flying bombing and transport missions from India to Burma or China over "the hump" - the Himalayas, the world's tallest mountain chain. These pilots faced enormous obstacles, starting with the Himalayas. Once the planes reached Burma, the jungle offered its own challenges for navigating and landing. These missions were considered the most dangerous and treacherous in the war.

Military commanders considered a flight over the CBI Hump to be more hazardous than a bombing mission over Europe. More than 1,300 pilots and crew members were lost, and more than 500 transport planes crashed trying to make it.

From looking at this guy and chatting with him, you would never know any of this. He was a humble man with a great sense of humor but never talked about his background.

I wish I knew more about him when I served under him. He was one of the many unsung heroes of World War II.

4

Transition

My time in the military set me up for a good management job in a mid-size company in the aerospace industry.

While in the Pentagon, I got to know a marketing rep from one of the contractors we dealt with. When he understood that I was going to leave the Air Force, he told me his company was looking for someone to fill a new position in the type of work I was doing.

He invited me to the company, and after a brief interview, they offered me the job. I reported directly to a company vice president. I realized I was a big fish in a small pond.

When I left the Air Force, my fiancé and I got married. We moved from Washington, D.C., to the company headquarters in the Midwest to follow my first job in industry in that mid-size company.

I had no trouble adapting my Air Force experience to the new environment in the private sector. Having coordinated with many Air Force organizations and across federal agencies while I was in the Pentagon served me well in my new position in industry.

I managed a small team responsible for support functions to company proprietary research and development (R&D) projects. We worked with approximately one hundred fifty employees. They were mostly scientists, physicists, mathematicians, and engineers of various types.

I interacted with many of these people daily. Some were outgoing, but most of them were stereotypical quirky introverts. Getting to know them was a challenge. And in many instances, the R&D folks were not happy with the requirements our team had to impose on them for proprietary information security and operations. For example, because of the competitive sensitivity of our proprietary material, documents and drawings had to be stamped with proprietary markings, accounted for, and stored in locked cabinets.

While I had the authority to direct that these requirements be implemented, I knew authoritarianism was not a feasible way to do things and people would object. We needed them to willingly accept these restrictions and implement them. I had to sell them on the idea that implementing security requirements was a necessity for us to do business. During the initial security briefings of everyone who came into our proprietary programs, I showed them comparisons of what we were doing against what other competing companies were doing. I explained the relative value of contracts if we won competitions for business. These explanations made implementing our requirements more palatable to them.

The bottom line was that if we were not able to protect our information and innovations, we would not be able to compete for business. And it was imperative that I see things from their perspective and how implementing security requirements would affect their work. Eventually, they appreciated my perspective.

Please pass the potatoes.

This was a great experience for me to get my feet wet in managing in the private sector. Even though the management hierarchy was like the Air Force, there was a more casual and informal atmosphere in how people worked together.

This position also gave me the opportunity to interact more with my counterparts in the industry. This would be most valuable later when I represented the next company in an industry aerospace association.

This was the first time in my career that I had to manage political situations. I worked quite closely with our chief engineer, our directors of marketing and strategy, and our business manager.

We all reported to our vice president.

Except for the business manager, my relationships with them were exceptionally good. They accepted me and my position and knew that what I did supported them and their teams.

But the business manager was another story.

One of my early challenges happened almost immediately on my first day on the job. The business manager cornered me in the hallway. He was a short, stocky, broad-shouldered man with a square head. He wore black horn-rimmed glasses. He tried to project the air of authority but couldn't quite pull it off. His style was abrupt, and he always spoke in a loud, staccato fashion in an attempt to convey the "authority" he didn't have. Although he was competent at what he did, he was not well-liked by his own staff or the rest of the executives.

He braced me up again the wall, looked up at me glowering, and in a raspy voice with great exasperation, he said, "Listen, Jed, I know you report to the VP, but I want you to know that I am lobbying for you to work for me. Your function, in my view, is a business management function, and I intend to give you direction on what you should be doing."

This confrontation was unnerving, but I didn't take it seriously, knowing that because of the type of work I was doing, I had to report to the person in the highest position in the organization, without being filtered by anyone else. My challenge was to work with him despite his attitude.

During my entire time with the company, he did his best to sabotage and discredit me and my efforts. His attempts failed, but I found it a very uncomfortable situation to have to constantly deal with and worry about. I did what I could to get along with him. I always gave him an early heads-up on things I would propose that could affect his business responsibilities. I went out of my way to consider and incorporate his comments wherever I could. Approaching him this way helped me to maintain a "reasonable" working relationship in spite of his efforts against me.

I also had a counterpart responsible for implementing government requirements for handling Department of Defense (DoD) classified contracts. Our responsibilities were similar but separate. Like the business manager, my counterpart who managed DOD classified material in the company felt that I should report to him, but at least he was friendly, and we made peace and coexisted without problems.

5

A Way to Relate

Throughout this first experience in private industry, I continued to learn more about how to manage myself in dealing with people. I learned to establish my mindset when I meet someone. I still use this highly effective process.

To do this, I find something I sincerely like about a person I meet. It could be their hair color or eyes, what they are wearing, their tone of voice, or their posture. It doesn't matter what it is. What matters is that I can identify something pleasant I sincerely like about that person. I say to myself, "I like you." When I do this, my approach to him or her is warm and caring. And they always respond well.

Physiologically, my eyes and pupils are wide and inviting, my shoulders relaxed, the tone of my voice soft, and the language I use positive. I lean toward them to speak, giving them my full attention, and my body language therefore is open and non-threatening.

These methods are very effective, and I have learned that, for the most part, people resonate with how you approach them. They respond in kind. Setting my mindset to expect their favorable responses has been a great technique to connect with anyone in the most positive way.

The bottom line is that I can consciously decide to take the lead and how I want to act with and respond to others. I can manage my attitude for the best outcomes.

When I act in this way—sensitive, open, and inviting—my relationships with others can be exceptionally positive. When we disagree, it can be with honesty, openness, and respect. And, even in somewhat confrontational situations, using this means to connect has helped maintain and often improve relationships.

But nothing is ever 100% effective. There is always an exception to every rule. Sometimes, relationships don't work out, even if you've given your best effort. You just have to accept what they are and move on.

Please pass the potatoes.

Takeaway

A Way to Relate

- Trust yourself to reach out to another person when you meet him or her. In your approach, convey sincerity, openness, caring, and respect.
- Find something you sincerely like about that person: a physical feature, voice, speaking accent, bearing, clothing, any other characteristics, but it must be something you sincerely like.
- When you do this and find and express what you like, unconsciously and naturally your approach to that person will be warm and caring.
- He or she will usually react in kind, setting up a positive relationship to build good communication and developing respect and trust, as you do.
- Even if you disagree, conversations can be amicable, and results can be more positive.

Introspection

A Way to Relate

Think about a couple of people you respect and with whom you have a good relationship.

- List the things you like about them and why you have a good connection.
- In listing these items, how does it make you feel? What emotions does this list elicit?

Now consider a person with whom you have a less-than-good relationship that you would like to improve.

- Does this relationship not work well? Is there anxiety or tension between you two? Can you communicate the cause of the tension? If there is, identify it and work to eliminate it.
- Who is more responsible for this discord? You or the other person? Why?

Consider applying the positive aspects of your good relationships to this less-than-positive one.

- If you change your attitude, could you improve this less-than- good relationship?
- What would be the signs that this relationship is improving? On your part? On their part?

Expected Outcome: Gain a broadened perspective on how a positive mindset toward others and non-verbal interaction can positively affect your relationships.

6

The Next Big Move

There were a number of reasons I was excited about my first job in industry in the Midwest after the Air Force. Having met a number of the key people in my new company organization during my job interview, I knew I would be working with people who were competent, professional, friendly, and who would support me in my job. And moving to a new location would be a refreshing and exciting experience.

I got to know several of the executives at the company and enjoyed my relationships with them.

Interestingly, a relationship with one of them would lead to an unusual situation where I helped him get a better job and, subsequently, he did the same for me.

He was the key strategist for our organization and a quiet guy with a great sense of humor. Although he was about fifteen years my senior, we became fast friends.

His job was strategizing "next moves" for how we marketed our R&D products, primarily to DoD. He always came up with refreshing and innovative marketing plans.

I marveled at how he worked. I would pass by his office routinely to see him sitting at his desk with an unlit cigar in his mouth. He would be either reading an historical book on war strategy or musing at notes he had written on his whiteboard. After a while, he would slowly get up from his desk, take a marker, and add or modify the notes on his whiteboard, then go back to his desk and muse some more. Eventually, he came up with full-blown strategy papers on how we could market our next offerings to potential customers.

He was highly regarded. Several years earlier, he had been tapped by executives in the CIA to take a leave of absence from the company and join them in strategic planning. He did this periodically, spending a year in the government and then returning to the company.

When I was with the company for a couple of years, he approached me about wanting to move to a larger company where his services could be used to a greater extent. With my contacts in the contractor community, I was able to introduce him to people in a much larger company on the West Coast. Six months later, he was offered a VP position in that company's advanced projects division, and he left us.

Not long after he got situated on the West Coast, he called me. "Jed," he said, "the company is looking for someone to groom and move up the ladder in their security organization. They need you here." He put me in contact with the right people for a visit and an interview. The Corporate Director of Security and Fire Protection interviewed me.

Control of company-sensitive and government classified information were responsibilities of his organization, as were company internal investigations and the uniformed security and firefighting organizations. It was a large organization, with about 500 employees on three shifts in several administrative and manufacturing sites.

There was plenty of room for me to grow.

In my interview, the Director said, "Jed, with your background in information protection, I want to start you out working as an individual contributing manager in our control of DoD classified and our internal Advanced Projects (AP) sensitive information. You will report to two managers, one in each of these areas. As you progress, I want to move you around into broader responsibilities. If you continue to be successful, I intend to groom you to take on my position in a few years."

Once again, I was stunned by what potentially lay ahead for me. And yes, just a little bit fearful, but by this time I had learned to control any fear I might have when new challenges presented themselves.

I accepted the position, and my wife and I moved to the West Coast, where my challenging new job awaited at the company headquarters.

As soon as I arrived. I looked up and reconnected with my friend from the Midwest, whom I had helped get his job in the West Coast company and who connected me to my new job. On several occasions, we had the opportunity to work with each other again. He and I and our wives became good friends and stayed connected until his passing years later.

7

Back to Basics

With my prior experience in the Air Force and the smaller company in the Midwest, I was well versed in handling government classified and company sensitive information. Even with that, getting used to another company's systems and procedures was new and challenging.

To top that off, I was no longer managing people nor reporting to executive management as I had in previous positions. I was now a "novice" individual contributor with several other "Security Administrators" in a bullpen environment. All the perks that came with my previous job, like a reserved parking space, a large private office with mahogany furniture, and a private secretary, were gone, but I was okay with that. I was in a new, refreshing environment and excited to learn about it and connect with new people.

As Security Administrators, our job was to assist and monitor line employees and managers in handling company and classified information. Each of us was assigned specific project areas to support.

Our Information Security Program had four elements: standard DoD security, DoD special projects security, company AP security, and company commercial proprietary sensitive information security.

As I saw it, my job was to listen and soak up every bit of information I could. I consciously did not compare my situation to my previous jobs.

It was exciting to learn new material. I became a student of others who were masters of the trade in the company. This included my manager and the other Security Administrators from whom I learned a great deal.

Working simultaneously for two managers was very challenging. Each of them demanded my full-time effort. Each had a unique personality with completely different management styles. It was a real juggling act to satisfy them both.

In the DoD world, the manager I worked for understood my situation and helped groom me. He was a small, elf-like man with a great smile. He took me under his wing and guided me in the company systems for handling DoD classified and company proprietary material.

He had been with the company for years and was well known in DoD and industry circles as a subject matter expert in the requirements and rationale for handling classified material. My "home" desk with the other Security Administrators was in his area.

For the AP security job, I traveled three to four days a week to another company location, about forty five minutes from my home base, to work half days.

The AP security manager was a buffoon. He was flashy and dressed like he was on the fifth tee of the golf course- always with bright red or turquoise blue pants, casual patterned shirts, and brown and white saddle shoes. He had a thick head of unnaturally dark jet-black hair. There was no doubt it was a dye job. A thin black pencil mustache completed his laughable look. He was self-centered and lazy, and spent most of his time glad-handing our AP customers but didn't do much else.

He was hired a year before I arrived and didn't know how to manage. Those of us who worked for him did our jobs and rarely interfaced with him. When he did communicate with us, it was to criticize what we did, but he never followed through with any constructive guidance. No one respected him, including the customers we supported.

As I mentioned parenthetically at the conclusion of Chapter 5, not every relationship is salvageable. That was the case here. It was obvious that this manager had no intent to collaborate with or support those of us who reported to him. He was one of the very few people I worked with in my career with whom I could not develop a good relationship. It was truly a "grin and bear it" situation.

Why he was hired, I will never know. He lasted another year before he was fired.

8

Expanded Responsibilities

During my first couple of years, I continued to work in the two separate information security environments as an individual contributor manager.

Then I was promoted to managing our teams of Security Administrators in our DoD and Special Projects activities. Three managers and their teams of two to four Security Administrators reported to me. For the Special Projects efforts, our teams resided in each project's secure facilities.

We were audited annually by an inspection team from the Defense Investigations Service (DIS) to assess our company's handling of the standard DoD classified information. Their team was typically four special agents who looked at every aspect of how we handled DoD Confidential and Secret classified material. Their audits lasted about three weeks. They did a thorough job—reviewing our internal inspection records, tracing the accountability of classified material, how the material was stored and securely destroyed, when need be, and many other things.

We were also audited annually by a separate group of government inspectors from the program offices for DoD Special Projects for compliance with similar but slightly different requirements from standard DoD classified material. We had three to five special projects for manufacturing and R&D activities at any time in several of our company locations.

I oversaw all these inspections. Except for minor inconsistencies mentioned in the inspection reports, all went well. (Of course, to justify their existence, the inspectors had to find and report some discrepancies. Fortunately, none of these were ever major issues.)

These inspections became routine, but each held anxious moments for me and with no guarantee that they would be concluded favorably.

Even though there were numerous employees involved who were interviewed by the inspectors and I could not control the interviews or their outcomes, I always felt that my credibility weighed in the balance of how well these inspections turned out. After all, I was the point person for the company in these inspections, and how well they ended up would be attributed to me.

In addition, I was given the responsibility of developing the policy and operating procedures for our first internal company computing security program. This was in the early days of computing, with large-scale computers, raised-floor temperature-controlled data centers, and computer tape libraries. (Looking back, cumbersome to say the least.)

I built a small organization to lay out the aspects of the program and developed a computing security manual, including audit guidelines. To build the organization, I relied on the opinions of others in the computing business whom I trusted to recommend people they felt would fit in with us and our mission.

Once we had all this coordinated and established, we set out to assist in implementing these requirements across the company and then eventually to bring in an audit team to monitor implementation.

For continuity of this program, I was also designated as the Security and Fire Protection focal point to the company's computing division. Several times a week, I spent late afternoons at this division's complex assisting with any support they needed from Security and Fire Protection. I coordinated with line and executive managers on our organization's behalf and became good friends with many of them.

This was a different and refreshing aspect of my job. I relished being able to offer and fulfill other people's requests for service. The position was especially enjoyable because before me the computing division had never had a Security and Fire Protection contact to listen or help with what they needed. As I did, the folks with whom I dealt in the computing division appreciated our relationship, and they always gave me high marks for supporting them.

Although I did not realize it at the time, these relationships would eventually save my career in the company.

9

Unusual Assignments

Occasionally, the director asked me to do special assignments for him outside my regular job. These were unusual and interesting. Giving me these tasks showed the director's confidence that I could handle sensitive assignments.

Typically, they were investigative assignments, requiring me to research material, interview people, and report back to the director through brief memos stamped with proprietary "Company Sensitive" warnings. These assignments usually had very short turnaround times.

I also found somewhat perplexing, the director's admonitions not to ask how he would use my reports. He said the less I knew about what I investigated, the better. He explained that if I was ever called to testify in court or in a deposition, I needed to be able to truthfully say that I did not know anything beyond the tasks I reported on. This was a way to protect me and give me plausible deniability, he said. I admired him for his foresight but also wondered what I'd gotten myself into.

Over time, I was given the added responsibility to review, coordinate, and revise the procedures for handling and protecting company sensitive proprietary information. This job included determining the sensitivity level of information with each creator and how to mark, store, and properly dispose of it.

I interfaced routinely with our company commercial managers, research and development staffers, and the salesforce in handling this material. After a while, I became the de facto "subject matter expert" in handling company sensitive material.

In one instance, this new expertise led to a unique assignment. Once again, the director asked to see me. He explained, "I have been working with our corporate attorneys on a significant case of copyright infringement. We are suing one of our subcontractors for having used some of our proprietary drawings, duplicating our parts, and selling them to other companies as their own."

He continued, "We are at that stage of the suit where we are being asked to prove that we protect our company sensitive information as we say we do. Jed, I need you to meet with our attorneys and prepare to be deposed on this subject on our behalf."

I don't recall the exact amount in this case, but the suit involved millions of dollars.

This situation was scary. I felt a massive weight and enormous responsibility as a critical contributor to the suit's success. As I had done before, I had to muster my confidence and beat down the fear of failure.

I met with four of our corporate attorneys numerous times. In our initial meeting, they explained the background of the case and our company's position and strategy.

During our hours-long sessions, which were often grueling, they coached me on presenting myself and what to say and not say during the deposition.

They said, "We will be in an adjacent room to the court with you, as will two opposing company attorneys and a court reporter.

"Everything their attorneys ask and your responses will be recorded for use in the trial.

"When we are done with the process, you will be allowed to read your interview transcript and make any comments that you and we decide need to be made. Any changes we want to make need to be discussed with and agreed to by the other company's attorneys present with us. After this, we will all sign your deposition, and it will be entered into the court record as your official testimony. You will also be given a copy of the deposition."

"Okay, so far?" they asked. Very uncomfortably, I nodded yes.

The attorneys had more to say.

"Their attorneys may attempt to get close to you. They may try to get you to relax with questions like 'How is your day going?' or 'Was there much traffic coming over here?' Any small talk to make you feel comfortable with them. Just be polite but remain professional and don't buy any overtures by them.

"Be mindful to specifically answer only what they ask you. Answer in straightforward statements. If you can answer 'yes,' or 'no,' that is preferable. Beyond that, brief and precise statements are best. Don't add anything to expand your answers unless specifically asked, and if you are not sure, look to us, and we will guide you."

Our first meeting concluded with our attorneys telling me "We don't anticipate that you will have to take the stand in court."

I don't deny it—I was scared. But I tried to take in everything they told me.

In subsequent meetings, our attorneys gave me specific details of the infringements we were suing for. Most importantly, we rehearsed and role-played questions I might be asked and how to respond. In these sessions, our attorneys were abrupt and pointed in questioning me. They were almost aggressive toward me. But I realized that's how they had to be to prepare me for the other side's aggressiveness.

As unsettling as all this was, it helped me prepare for what I might be up against in the deposition.

I felt anxious, even fearful. I told our attorneys, "I can authoritatively testify about our company policy and procedures for handling company sensitive material, but I am shaky about how consistently we implement them."

"Implementation is out of Security's hands. That is up to each organization," I said.

They asked, "Doesn't Security audit organizations for proper material handling?"

"Yes," I replied, "We do, but only a small representative number of organizations and sporadically. With our finite resources and other responsibilities, the company is too big for us to audit every organization."

I continued, "Even then, unlike with the handling of government classified material, our findings of company sensitive material in handling irregularities are written as recommendations to the heads of the organizations, not as requirements."

They thought for a moment and looked at each other. Then one said, "If this comes up in the deposition, we will handle the answers."

What a relief!

The deposition lasted four hours. Most of the questions asked of me related to policy and procedure. To my surprise, the opposing attorneys were inexperienced in proprietary and company sensitive material handling or security implementation. I was able to answer their questions easily to their satisfaction and credited the thorough preparation I had been given.

When it was over, I felt like we had dodged a bullet. The opposing attorneys were inept in their questioning.

The case went to a negotiated settlement in our favor, and a trial was averted. I was told by our attorneys that my testimony played a significant role in our win! Another relief, and I was very grateful.

10

Leading National Action

The National Industrial Security Program (NISP)

Because of my management responsibilities, I was able to see the myriad of security requirements the government levied on us in industry across the spectrum of typical DoD classified programs and Special Projects. And, from my Air Force career, I also had a good understanding of handling Top Secret code-word material.

As I said before, these systems had their own requirements. They were similar but varied somewhat from each other. The result was that in these areas the government and industry had to implement slightly different requirements for every aspect of their security programs. In some cases, compartmented projects administered by the same government oversight organization had different security requirements, but for no apparent reasons.

The dilemma was an immense frustration for those of us administering government security programs in industry. More so, there was a significantly high cost to implement different requirements. And, of course, the unnecessary cost was reflected in contract costs to the government.

Our company was a member of the Aerospace Industries Association (AIA). It was a lobbying organization comprising about 250 companies that did business with DoD. They ranged from airframe manufacturers to computing companies, aluminum and other raw material providers, and electronics companies. AIA represented every industrial element of products produced for DoD.

One of the advantages of my last job in Information Security, which I held for several years, was getting to know my counterparts in other companies. Because of this, I was asked to represent the company in the Industrial Security Committee of AIA.

Shortly after joining it, I was asked to chair the Industrial Security Committee and held the chairmanship for three consecutive annual terms. This was unprecedented.

Along with security managers and directors from other companies, I was frustrated with the inconsistencies and unnecessary duplication of the security requirements levied on us by DoD and other federal agencies our companies dealt with. These often wasted time, money, and manpower for both private industry and the government itself.

To address these problems, I proposed that the AIA Industrial Security Committee launch our own study on this subject and coordinate our findings with our government counterparts. The target was to develop and implement one security protocol that would be adhered to by all federal agencies and departments that we all did business with.

We coined a name for this project: "The National Industrial Security Program (NISP)." This was a ground-breaking initiative. At the beginning of this effort, the Executive Board of the Industrial Security Committee asked me to chair the NISP Committee and to be the face of the NISP to the Federal Government and industry. Fifteen of us security professionals were on the NISP Committee from the various AIA member companies. Except for me the other members were corporate directors of security for their respective companies.

Once again, I was in rarified air. Our task was to connect with the government security directors in each of the Federal Government departments and agencies to join in our efforts and to accompany me to brief their agency and department heads on the program.

My company was in total support of our efforts. So much so that they paid for us to produce a summary video, which we circulated through the government and industry. It captured the essence of the NISP, its background, and detailed costs gathered by AIA and DoD on the duplication of security requirements. I developed the content for the video, directed it, and managed its production and dissemination in the government and industry.

For three years, a group of us coordinated the NISP through AIA. I spoke at security conferences across the country on the program and detailed our progress. And I'm happy to say that the NISP received resounding support from across the industry.

A small group of us met with the directors of security for each of the Federal Government agencies, departments, and military services to brief them on the program, involve them in decision making for it, and gain their support. This immersion allowed them to pre-brief their agency heads, take credit for their involvement, and arrange for us to collectively brief their bosses for their approval. The security directors were able to take ownership of a program that would significantly benefit their organizations and the government. It was an all-around win.

It was exhilarating and challenging to be leading this Committee, working with directors of security in the aerospace industry, and also coordinating with the highest level of security directors and department and agency heads in the Federal Government. I was very proud of what we were accomplishing and my having initiated this program and leading the charge.

Please pass the potatoes.

I frequently traveled to Washington, D.C. to brief heads of departments and agencies. Some notable briefings were with the directors of the CIA, the FBI, the NSA, the Secretaries of Treasury, DoD, Commerce, and Transportation, each of the military services, and the Deputy Secretary of State.

On several occasions, I traveled from the West Coast to D.C. for an hour-long meeting and turned around and flew home.

I traveled so much to D.C. that the hotel I stayed at knew me by name and always reserved the room I preferred. Each time I checked in, they called me by name and asked if I wanted my "usual" meal delivered to my room on my first night.

As we moved along the process of working toward a Presidential Executive Order to implement the NISP, the administrative assistant in my organization started and updated what wound up to be a small telephone-book-size record of all our meetings, with details of who attended, dates and times, issues discussed, outcomes reached, and agreements made to support the program.

Twice a year, I briefed company presidents and their executive staffs of AIA companies at their semi-annual meetings and provided them with an update on our collective efforts. I gave each of them our updated "telephone book" document. We were applauded for our initiative and the cost savings that could be realized from implementation of the NISP.

I also maintained weekly contact with the President's National Security Advisor, General Brent Scowcroft, through a Rear Admiral on his staff.

At one point, we needed President Bush to sign a promotional letter that we could circulate for the program. I recall the Admiral telling me he had handed the letter to General Scowcroft, who gave it to the President to sign while he was attending a barbeque party.

In my working closely with DoD, their budgetary staff estimated that the savings across government agencies and departments in implementing the NISP would be **five billion dollars** a year by reducing the duplication of security programs levied on industry.

They estimated the cost saving to industry was four times that amount.

The program culminated in Presidential Executive Order 12829, signed by President Bush in 1993. It was turned over to the Clinton Administration to implement. This effort was a resounding success. The program still exists. The following are the key elements of this important, money-saving program.

"The National Industrial Security Program (NISP) was established by Executive Order 12829 to ensure that cleared U.S. defense industry safeguards the classified information in their possession while performing work on contracts, programs, bids, or research and development efforts.

The Defense Counterintelligence and Security Agency (DCSA) administers the NISP on behalf of the Department of Defense and 34 other federal agencies. There are approximately 12,500 contractor facilities that are cleared for access to classified information under DCSA's security oversight responsibilities. DCSA provides field personnel, Government Contracting Activities (GCAs) and cleared contractors with timely, consistent policy guidance and to provide effective interpretation of the NISP." (Wikipedia)

Areas covered by the NISP include:
- Security Clearances
- Facility Clearances
- Personnel Security Clearances
- Foreign Ownership, Control, or Influence (FOCI)
- Security Training and Briefings
- Classification and Marking
- Safeguarding Classified Information
- Visits and Meetings
- Subcontracting
- Information System Security
- Special Requirements
- RD and FRD
- DoD Critical Nuclear Weapon Design Information (CNWDI)
- Intelligence Information
- Communication Security (COMSEC)
- International Security Requirements
- Miscellaneous Information
- TEMPEST (requirements for preventing electronic emanations)
- Defense Technical Information Center (DTIC)
- Independent Research and Development (IR&D) Efforts

After President Bush signed the Executive Order, our CEO invited me to his office for coffee and gave me a $10,000 check as a thank-you bonus for leading the Program.

This success was, of course, satisfying. But ironic. Shortly after, my trajectory in the company took a nosedive. (More in Chapter 13.)

11

MORE SIGNIFICANT ASSIGNMENTS

Just before the onset of the NISP project, I was promoted to Senior Manager and given the responsibility for the Security and Fire Protection organizations supporting two different locations. Both had active company airfields and manufacturing facilities. I headed the first organization for two years. Then I was moved to the second, larger organization, where I stayed for another several years until I left Security and Fire Protection. Both organizations operated on three shifts, twenty-four hours a day.

To stay connected with our employees, I periodically staggered my work shift to be on the first shift, the latter part of the first shift into the mid-second shift, and the latter part of the third shift into the first shift. Those who have worked in organizations with different shifts recognize that each shift has its own culture.

Even though this schedule was sometimes tough on my biological clock, it was something I enjoyed the most in my job. It made a big difference to our people to know that I was willing to meet with them face-to-face at their work sites regardless of their shift.

Before I started this process, I sat down with all our managers and explained that my purpose was to get to know our operations and our people on every shift. I made sure to tell them that I wasn't spying on our folks, looking over our managers' shoulders, or judging them but rather to become acquainted with them and be available. It took a little while before the managers and our hourly employees trusted me but my presence helped to build and maintain high morale. They knew that I cared enough to visit them in person.

No other senior manager had ever visited each shift as I did. The grapevine chatter I heard was that our hourly security and fire protection employees sincerely appreciated my visits.

Since many of my daily responsibilities were with first-shift operations, I typically worked a complete first shift in addition to the split shifts.

I was extremely fortunate that our organizations' managers were consummate professionals. I was always proud of the fact that 90% of our security officers and all our firefighters, including the management chain, were Emergency Medical Technicians (EMTs). Their expertise and dedication served us well because most of our emergency calls were for accidents on the airfields or in manufacturing areas.

In addition to managing these organizations—through a great group of mid and line managers and hourly employees, I served as the primary liaison for the Security and Fire Protection organization to the executives in the operating divisions we supported. From time to time, with two other senior managers, I also served as our deputy director.

As I mentioned earlier, our director also designated me as organization liaison for the company computing division for anything the division needed from Security and Fire Protection. Little did I know this position would be very helpful to me several years later when my time in Security and Fire Protection was unceremoniously brought to an end.

12

COMPETITION AND WINNING AND LOSING

We live in a society that emphasizes competition and winning from early childhood. In school, children are encouraged to excel, to "win," but often, this is promoted as competition with oneself to do the best one can. In juvenile sports, "winning" is couched in focusing on the team, winning by working together. This emphasis continues into adolescence and adulthood.

In business and social settings, healthy competition is a good thing, when individuals and groups compete toward specific goals and objectives. But competition can be detrimental when it is a negative or destructive focus aimed toward individuals.

Winning often takes the form of competing for promotions, higher pay, better working conditions, and recognition. These goals are typically sought reasonably within the framework of ethical and professional business norms. Undercutting others to get ahead is normally not condoned nor tolerated. It is frowned upon.

But if winning is obsessive, and at "all costs," it can devolve into winning at the expense of others. If so, the win may be a hollow victory and it will damage relationships, one's reputation, and one's ability to work congenially in teams and within organizations.

Among the many organizations with which I worked, I saw that the least successful ones were those where the internal ethos was an overzealous, unhealthy "win" attitude or a "win at all costs" competitive attitude at the expense of others.

In these organizations, the employee morale was terribly low, and the organizations were unable to keep qualified, motivated people. Even though their attrition was high, the negative ethos of these groups did not change until management eventually realized that the competitive focus was causing the organization to fail.

My exposure to these organizations and thinking about their failures led me to several conclusions. If you are conscious of the harm that compulsive competition and "winning at all costs" can do, you can halt it, and hopefully turn it around, before it gets so out of control. It's not that wanting to win gets you. It's when winning is the only thing that matters. The compulsion is the trap.

Losing is the other side of winning. For some situations, losing is inevitable and a fact of life. Not all activities or relationships can be winning propositions.

And sometimes, winning or losing is not in your control. As you will see more in this story, I have experienced both.

Whatever the situation, avoid the tendency to disparage yourself or to consider yourself a loser, or ruminate on the reason for losing. This advice is easy to give but often difficult to follow.

Taken in the right light, losing can be fertile grounds for learning and growing. One can learn from the factors that precluded winning and help to build on them toward future wins.

As I thought about all this and was making my way through my career, what became a constant in my thinking was that how I managed myself was the key to everything. Then I didn't have to worry about winning or losing.

If I considered others with humility and seriously respected and listened to them (elements of what I began to call "we first,"), it worked well. We all collaborated well, and we produced great results.

In the few times when my ego got the best of me and I was tuned out to others, only thinking in my own best interest (what I coined as "me first,"), the relationships fell apart. And little got done.

I learned to listen to myself and to question what motivated me. Was it all to get ahead, focused primarily on "me first" for only what was good for me and potentially at the expense of others? Or were my actions and interests truly to support our workers and our organization's collective goals and accomplishments for the good of us all, "we first"?

I learned to really listen to others—to truly hear them, and not just bide my time until I could weigh in with my own two cents.

I also learned the value of respecting others and the importance of trusting. I realized the power of collaborating toward common goals and how much more we could accomplish as a supportive team rather than operating as individuals.

Takeaway

Winning and Losing

- If hard and compulsive win-lose is a central focus, it can be destructive. Nothing about it is a win for anyone involved.
- This reinforces extreme competition among everyone, and nobody wins.
- Collegiality and allegiance to a common cause are not possible.
- This perpetuates negative communication and mistrust.
- Focus on organizational and individual needs for collective success is impossible.

Introspection

Winning and Losing

This exercise may help you become aware of and deal with an environment in which extreme win-lose is the prevailing attitude.

- Consider a setting in which win-lose is a major element.

Ask yourself why this exists:

- Is it inadvertent? Is it promoted by whomever is in charge?
- Why? For what reasons?
- What effects does this outlook have on teaming and focus for positive results?
- What can you think of to dissipate and change this focus for a more inclusive, positive environment?
- What actions can you take to make this happen?

<u>Expected Outcome:</u> Understanding that serious "win-lose" is all lose and of no benefit to anyone involved.

Takeaway

Destructive Extreme Competitiveness

- A healthy competitive work environment can increase production, efficiency, focus, employee motivation, and results.

- On the other hand, "dog-eat-dog" competition can create a stressful, pressure-packed environment that promotes fighting among employees, hindering work quality, and negatively affecting employee self-esteem and sense of well-being.

- Extreme internal competition breeds mistrust and suspicion of others. Trust and positive, appreciative, and respectful relationships are needed.

- Competition can destroy the environment needed to work together for common purpose.

- When employees compete, they are choosing not to support each other. Someone will "win," and someone will "lose." In truth, everyone will lose because they will fail to see the unique value that each person can contribute to satisfy common needs and to reach the group's shared goals.

- Relying on or allowing extreme internal competition to be the foundation to reach positive ends is inconsistent and will not work. One cannot use a negative means and expect to have positive outcomes.

Introspection

Destructive Competitiveness

Think about an individual with whom you are competing, either someone in your professional life, a peer, someone who reports to you or someone to whom you report, or someone in your personal life, such as your spouse or partner, a parent, or a sibling.

- Admit to yourself that you feel competitive with this person by identifying and writing down the characteristics of your interaction. (e.g., mistrust, suspicion, withholding of information, argumentativeness, stress).

- Write down your view of the basis for feeling competitive with this person.

- Was it something this person did or said? Was it something you did? How long ago?

- If you are precipitating the competition, what are you doing? Or what did you do? How does/did this person react to what you do/did?

- If it is your view that the other person is precipitating this competitiveness, what is he/she doing, and how do you react to it?

- Think about and write down what negative impacts and implications this competitive relationship has for you and the group you and the other person are members of.

- How does this competition affect you?

- How does this competition affect the other members of the group?

- What could you do to reduce the competitiveness of this relationship? How would you approach and discuss this with the other person?
- Commit to taking the steps you described above to reduce this conflict and competition.
- Once you have taken the steps, review how you feel about the actions and reactions of the other person. Review what effects this change has for the members of the group.
- Discuss the positive aspects of the changes in the relationship with the person with whom you had been competing, so you can both now work with the common goal of reducing your mutual competitiveness.
- Build on the positive aspects of your relationship to continue to strengthen it.

<u>Expected Outcome:</u> Understanding competition and developing each person's consciousness to dissipate inappropriate behavior.

13

The Balloon Bursts

I was thoroughly enjoying my job managing our security and fire protection operations organizations. Everything seemed to be in balance for me in my career progression. Unfortunately, during this time, my mentor, who had taken over as the Director of Security and Fire Protection and to whom I reported, contracted pancreatic cancer, and six months later passed away. This development had the unpleasant potential to throw off my trajectory in the organization. And I deeply felt the personal loss of my mentor's passing. He and I had become good friends.

An interim director was named, and the search for a permanent director was initiated. The search was interrupted when our company CEO attended a conference and met an assistant director of the FBI who was about to retire.

Our CEO must have been very impressed with him because, with little vetting, the CEO hired this person as our new Director of Security and Fire Protection. But he had no experience in our industry or knowledge about what our company or our security and fire protection organization did. So much for grooming and promoting from within!

Little did I know that this development was the beginning of my "downfall" and my unceremonious exit from the organization.

What became very clear early on was that this new director was more interested in promoting himself than managing the organization.

He spent much of his time socializing with executives in the company, leaving the day-to-day management activities to those of us who knew what we were doing. He set himself up in a lavish office and sat grandly behind his oversized desk but took little interest in the organization.

The people who reported directly to him, including me, had little to no respect for him. But because the company CEO had hired him, everyone feared calling him out. We knew too it wouldn't reflect well on us to "tattle" about him to our division VP or the CEO.

He had been on the job for about two weeks when I travelled to Washington, D.C., to brief Judge William Sessions, Director of the FBI, his former boss, on an update on the NISP. While enroute, I was told by one of our people that our new director was absolutely livid that I was briefing the FBI Director. Ironically, when I had this meeting, the FBI assistant directors who had been peers of my new boss stopped in to ask me to say hello to my boss when I returned to the office.

My meeting with Judge Sessions was supposed to last fifteen minutes, but we hit it off so well that we talked for an hour and a half. He had to keep telling his secretary to reschedule other appointments so we could continue our conversation.

I was buoyed by having been with the Director of the FBI! And I thought about it with great enjoyment on the flight home.

On my return to the office, our new director immediately called me into his office. From his comments, I knew he had received very positive feedback from his former FBI colleagues about my meeting with Judge Sessions, and he was less than happy about it.

Sitting behind his throne of a desk, and with a smile on his face, he said, "Jed, I appreciate what you are doing with the NISP, but as I see it, you and your notoriety are a threat to me."

Shell shocked!

He continued. "That said, you are going to have to either find another job in or outside the company, or I will have to fire you. I'll give you four weeks to find someplace to go."

My mind went blank. I couldn't believe what I had just heard and couldn't say a word. I got up and left.

He continued to smile as I left his office.

Very quickly, the big office, the lavish furniture, the reserved parking space, and all the other trappings of executive management I had enjoyed disappeared.

I was moved to the back of our building in a small cubicle in a windowless corner. I had an old beat-up and dented metal gray desk and one creaking chair.

My standing in the organization was stripped away from me. People stopped talking to me. Those whom I trusted, and who I thought would stand up for me shunned me. No one wanted to come to my aid because they were all afraid of our new director. Nobody would help me.

To my amazement, our division VP, with whom I had had a good rapport, also refused to help, and began ignoring me. It was obvious that he, too, was afraid to challenge the new director, even though the director reported to him.

It seemed as though everyone was in awe of this director because of his recent senior position in the FBI.

Two years after I left the organization, the company fired this director for incompetence, but not until he had ruined the careers of several of us whom he felt threatened him.

14

Fall Into Depression

I was paranoid. Despite continued success with a "we first" collaborative attitude up to this point in my career, I became a panicked "me first" competitive person. For the first time in my career, I was overwhelmingly concerned with self-preservation.

For some reason, while I was in my last weeks in the organization, I continued to be invited to our director's weekly executive management meetings.

In these weekly meetings, I was very nervous. Uncharacteristically, I always spoke first, loudly blurting out my opinions and often interrupting others mid-sentence. Other attendees quietly let me vent, then softly gave their views, mostly repeating what I had just said. But their voices were heard, and I was ignored.

Hey! Gimme those potatoes!!

Feeling a need to survive blinded me to everything I knew about relating to people. I recognized what I was doing but couldn't stop myself, trying to keep my head above water.

I was left on my own to try and find another job outside Security and Fire Protection. I felt completely isolated, with no idea what to do. My career seemed to be going up in a cloud of smoke.

I was in a horrible place, miserable and scared. I started to take my frustrations and fear of helplessness out on my family. Every day, I went home angry and lashed out at my wife and kids without the slightest provocation.

I couldn't sleep and felt that the pressure would overtake me. There were many nights when I expected I would not wake up the following morning but would die of a heart attack in the middle of the night.

I had to survive but had no clue how. I kept obsessing, asking myself how I would provide for my family. I was desperate.

I became seriously depressed. As much as I hate to admit it here, it felt like my career had suddenly ended, and I wasn't proud of how I was treating my family as a result of this frustrating situation. I was taking it out on them and felt useless. I began to think that they would be better off without me.

I knew I needed help to deal with this deepening depression, but I was afraid to get it. Because of the clearances I held, seeking psychiatric help could be grounds for revocation of my government clearances. That could end my career in Security.

I had the solution: suicide. That would fix my dilemma and free my family from how I treated them. They could move on without me.

I seriously planned my escape. I would sit in my car in the closed garage, turn on the classical guitar music I loved, roll down the car windows and turn on the ignition, and allow the fumes to overtake me and put me permanently to sleep.

I wrestled back and forth with this scenario. But, after much thought, I concluded that suicide was not the answer. Instead, I bit the bullet (maybe not the best metaphor) and went to see a clinical psychotherapist. When I described my situation to her, she was astounded that I was surviving.

Early on, she asked me to describe my childhood to her. Although I didn't understand why she asked, I told her.

"When I was fifteen," I said, "I watched my father die, unable to save him. He was always angry, with a short fuse and an explosive temper.

"He was home convalescing from an ulcer on the outside of his stomach. While it was painful, his doctor advised that it was not life-threatening and that he just needed rest. He had no choice but to stay in bed and try to relax. This gave him some peace away from the daily pressures he fell victim to at his work place.

"It was usual for him to come home angry and blow off steam by yelling at my sister and me.

"Routinely, for years, after I was supposed to be in bed asleep in my room, I would hear the muffled sounds of my parents fighting.

"On many occasions, I would hear the front door slam and the engine of our car start, knowing my father had sped away angry.

"I often heard my mom quietly crying in their bedroom after my father left in a huff. I lay in bed, wide awake and scared.

"He always came back, but sometimes in the morning, I could feel the tension between my parents from the fight the night before.

"But he calmed down when he became ill and was bedridden.

"When my father was home recuperating, my mother slept in the den to allow him to rest easily, so my father had their main bedroom to himself. "

I paused, thinking back, unconsciously fidgeting.

"I was not close to him until two weeks before he died. For his last two weeks, I would come home from school and sit by his bedside, talking about nothing. Those chats gave us time to bond."

(I will never forget those few marvelous days with my Dad.)

I continued my childhood story, as painful as it was to describe.

"At 3:05 a.m. on May 1, 1959, while lying half asleep. I heard a rumble across the hall in my parents' bedroom. I knew something was wrong. I jumped out of bed, ran into my parents' bedroom, and saw the light in their adjacent bathroom.

"I rushed in to find my father sitting on the floor in his bathrobe with his back propped up against the stall shower door. The glass door was cracked and broken with blood on it where he had fallen and slid down. He was unconscious with his eyes closed, breathing heavily with his swollen tongue out.

"I watched as he took his last breath.

"And he was gone. A massive heart attack."

I kept telling my story.

"My Dad died on a Friday morning. The next day, my mother, sister, and I were still reeling from the previous night, and the phone rang. I picked it up and answered it. The man on the other end was a close friend of my Dad's. He asked to speak to my Dad. I told him my Dad had died early in the morning the day before.

"He was so shocked that he had a heart attack and died holding the phone. I recall vividly hearing his wife screaming in the background as she saw him fall to the floor. Quietly I hung up the phone."

I closed my eyes and took a deep breath.

I said, "There I was, a fifteen-year-old kid, thinking that I was responsible for not saving my Dad from dying and causing the death of one of his friends. All in less than twenty-four hours."

The psychotherapist was riveted. She looked at me wide-eyed and began taking notes.

"My Dad died toward the end of my sophomore year in high school. The few months after he passed away were especially awkward for me. My friends avoided me not knowing what to say.

"I remember walking around a hall corner at school and overhearing two teachers say, 'Jed's doing fairly well, considering his handicap.'"

"That made me so angry! I was fuming. I said to myself, 'I don't have a handicap! Something happened to me out of my control, and I am suffering because of it!'

"It was that moment I vowed I would never let things happen to me that were out of my control. That was not rational to say, but since then, I have tried to control my destiny as much as possible."

I paused, then said, almost to myself—with a slight chuckle, "And here I am again trying to manage being out of control."

I had finished my story and looked down and stared at the floor in front of the psychotherapist. I felt defeated. We were both silent for a moment.

As I looked up, I saw her looking at me with sympathy.

Then she whispered, "Do you have a family album at home from when you and your sister were small children?"

This was an odd question not connected to anything we had been talking about, but I responded.

"Yes. I have one of those old wood-covered albums my mother gave me. It has our family name in script wood scroll fastened on the wood front cover diagonally with small round brass nails. It is bound with a leather thong. My mother chronicled our family history in it with old sepia family photos on black pages. She had written titles and comments with dates under each with a white fountain pen. The photos were held on the pages with the old style photo points on each corner."

The psychotherapist said, "I would like you to go home and look at that photo album. When we meet next week, I would like you to describe your feeling having spent time with those photos and the memories they bring back to you."

"Okay," I said, still not understanding the reason.

That evening, I went into the attic and found the photo album. I knew exactly where it was but hadn't thought to pick it up until now.

I sat quietly at our kitchen table and slowly thumbed through the pages, remembering some places we had been as a family—our happy times.

There was a wonderful picture of my sister on a pony at a summer camp, beaming joyfully like a Cheshire cat.

There was a picture of me as a six-year-old kid standing beside my Dad with his arm around me. We were both grinning.

There were group photos with relatives I didn't know. But for all of it, everyone was happy and smiling.

I spent three hours with that album, and when I was finished, I closed it and sat, still thinking back. Then, out of nowhere, I started crying. My sobs turned into inconsolable wailing. I cried and moaned and screamed and could not stop. It felt like I'd never climb out of that grief. I must have cried for thirty minutes.

When I was done, exhausted, I wiped the tears from my face but didn't move from the table. All my unconscious and hidden anger, fear, and guilt from what happened with my Dad were gone! Somehow, I felt refreshed, like a new person.

A few days later, I went back for what would be my last session with the psychotherapist. We discussed my experience with the photo album, and I said, "I think I am done. I appreciate everything you have helped me with, but I don't think I need to continue our sessions."

She strenuously objected, saying, "You have only been in these sessions with me for five weeks, and I would like to continue for at least another few months."

Again, I thanked her and left.

These sessions were invaluable to me. From then on, even though I still had no idea when or where I would get a job, I was excited to see what would happen next.

15

Safe Landing

I still had to land a new job, and time was ticking. The director was subtly putting constant pressure on me to leave, even though he had given me four weeks to find a job.

Although I was not as anxious as I had been about my predicament since my therapy sessions, I knew something had to pop to get me back on track in a career.

Looking for a new job outside the company and potentially relocating and uprooting my family did not sound like a good solution. But

nothing inside the company was on the horizon.

The word about my having to leave Security and Fire Protection was starting to get around the company. People I knew outside Security and Fire Protection with whom I had worked began to call or come by, and they were sympathetic about my situation. But none of them had ideas for where I could go.

Three weeks into my dilemma, I received a phone call from the Director of Technology in the computing services division of the company. I had known him for a while and worked with many of his staff. He said," I am sorry to hear about your problem, but I wanted to reach out and potentially offer you a job. Can you come over to my office tomorrow, and we can talk further?"

I was ecstatic and relieved. Trying to reign in my enthusiasm, I answered, "Yes, I would love to."

"How about 2:30?"

"I'll be there!"

I had no idea what he was thinking about the job, but I couldn't wait. This could be a real possibility.

Since we knew each other and I had worked closely with him in my role as the Security and Fire Protection liaison, and since I didn't know what he had in mind, I felt like there was nothing I had to prepare for. He knew me and my reputation, so I thought it would be a casual discussion.

Most of the computing division was housed in several buildings on its own campus. The buildings were only three years old, and the landscape architects had thoughtfully planted trees and put in an exercise path and walkways through a forested area. It was more like a park or a college campus than a business complex.

I joined him in his second floor office suite. As a director, he had a large, well-appointed corner office with expansive windows, a large wooden desk, and a small sofa and two stuffed chairs around a coffee table. It could easily have been someone's condo living room.

He was one of the people with whom I had coordinated as the Security and Fire Protection liaison to the computing division, so we knew each other and were comfortable with one another. We chatted casually for a few minutes, and then he got right into it.

"I am just the conduit for us to you," he said. I wasn't sure what he meant.

"You will be working directly for the VP of R&D, for whom I work, and the VP of Operations—both of whom I know you know pretty well.

"The position will be Senior Manager of Computing Security at the salary you have now, but of course, with growth potential. We expect you to start a small organization, helping the division implement the computing security requirements manual and auditing guidelines you established in Security and Fire Protection. Facilities has set up your office and an adjacent set of offices for the staff you will build, all of which will be next to the president's and vice president's executive suites. We'd like you to start as soon as you can. How does that sound?"

I was astounded and could barely get the words out. "That would be great! I can come over tomorrow and begin to set things up."

We stood up and shook hands.

"We are delighted to have you on the team," he said.

I almost ran to the parking lot, got in my car, and began yelling, "Yes, Yes, YES!!" at the top of my lungs.

I drove back to my small cubicle in the Security and Fire Protection complex.

Immediately, I threw the few items I had on my desk into a small box, tucked it under my arm, and walked to the director's complex. Then I approached his executive secretary.

She was what we called a "gatekeeper" for him—managing his calendar, answering the phone, and doing administrative functions.

She was an austere-looking woman in her early fifties, never married. She wore no makeup or jewelry and dressed in plain clothes as if she didn't want people to notice her. But, of course, everyone did.

She had been the director's executive secretary for at least the seventeen years I was in Security and Fire Protection. Although she didn't care for our current new director, she reluctantly stayed on to be able to retire in a couple of years.

It was known that nobody saw him without her approval. If you could not justify to her why you wanted to see him, you would almost surely be turned away or not be granted a later appointment with him. She quite literally ran the place and was a force to be reckoned with.

With all that, she and I got along well.

I said, "Hey, I wanted to let you know that I have vacated my cubicle. I am leaving permanently."

I handed her a slip of paper with my new phone number on it. "If you need anything from me you can reach me here."

She smiled a little and asked me where I was going. I was vague and told her just to one of the other divisions. I did not want to share any details.

I told her, "The director can read about it when the announcement is made in the company news bulletin on promotions and organizational changes."

She nodded and gave me another small smile. As I left, to my surprise she said she enjoyed working with me. I returned the sentiment.

Even though I had to work with Security and Fire Protection in my new position, I never again interfaced with the director nor visited his complex.

The wonderful lady who had been my secretary for most of my time in Security and Fire Protection was good enough to follow me to the new job in the computing division as our team administrative assistant.

In my new location, from time to time I was visited by uniformed folks with whom I had worked in Security and Fire Protection. We would reminisce and enjoy chatting. I always appreciated being remembered by them and looked forward to these visits.

16

New Beginning

My first meeting with the two VPs to whom I now reported was an upbeat, casual discussion. I had known both of them for some time because of my liaison function with the computing division when I worked for Security and Fire Protection. Their expectations of me and my expectations for the new job were totally in sync.

They gave me the limitations on how many new people I could hire, which included generous salary caps. I returned to my new office and began looking for some good employees to bring to our small team.

The folks we needed in our new team had to be good communicators, very people-oriented, and technically savvy, although we had serious "techies" at our disposal to help.

As with my other jobs, while we had the authority to direct our program's implementation, a sincere attitude of caring and helping would make things work.

To start our small organization, our administrative assistant suggested a young lady she knew with several years in the computing division. I interviewed her and hired her immediately.

She, in turn, knew two other folks qualified for what we needed.

The five of us set up shop. Our first order of business was to establish focal points through managers of the data centers around the division to implement our program. There were four data centers in our local area, two in the Midwest, two on the east coast, one in southern California, and one in Quebec, Canada.

Earlier, when I was fired from my senior management position in Security and Fire Protection, I could not have predicted that I would get an opportunity to start a new and vibrant organization, again breaking new ground in a project. This time I would implement innovative measures to help improve our computing security posture!

During our first meeting as a team, I expressed my pleasure and excitement in being together and emphasized that we were a team, each supporting the other to accomplish our common mission and purpose. I emphasized teaming and mutual support in each of the job interviews I conducted with our team members.

I stressed too that as a cohesive team, our mission was to engage computing centers across the division to educate them and engage them to want to implement the computing security requirements and audit guidelines. This familiarity was so they knew exactly what to expect and would get no surprises at the end of our audits.

Takeaway

Focus for Common Purpose

- Defining and agreeing on a group's shared purpose and focus will help everyone work together for exceptional results and aim for what is best for all.
- Each group member committing to act toward fulfilling the common purpose will help identify and resolve issues effectively.
- This behavior will help emphasize respect among members and appreciation for the value each person can contribute to fulfilling the group's shared objectives and goals.

Please pass the potatoes.

Introspection

Focus for Common Purpose

Consider the following in a group meeting:

- Does the group have a stated common purpose? Has it been discussed and agreed to by all in the group? If so, good. If not, start the dialogue for a common purpose to be defined and agreed on. Have it written down and distributed.

- Think about the value that each group member brings to the group and its common purpose. Write these down.

- Write down your view of what you believe you bring to the group.

- Suggest (and help start) dialogue in the group about what value each person brings to the group. Start by example and enunciate what you believe another group member brings to the group.

- Suggest the following exercise to start this dialogue:

- Have the group name a facilitator from within the group to lead this exercise. (The facilitator will lead the rest of this exercise.)

- Have each member of the group think about the value that each member brings to the group. Have them write down the name of every other group member on a separate piece of paper or card.

- On each of these cards, each member should list five things they believe that group member contributes to the group.

- When this part is completed for each group member, have the cards given to the facilitator.

- The facilitator will group all the cards by each member's name and then read aloud to the group what the group believes each member brings to the group.
- The facilitator will then provide each member with cards written about them to keep and think about.
- After completing the above exercise, observe if you feel there is now a closer, more respectful aura among the group members.
- If you think there is, why do you think it exists now and didn't before?
- If you think it doesn't exist, why not?
- Do you feel closer to others in the group?
- Suggest to the facilitator that the above questions be posed to the group and be discussed.

<u>Expected Outcome:</u> Developing a closer, respectful, and supportive relationship among team members.

17

Audits

A key part of my new job was to go out with my Security Administrators and perform security compliance audits at the computing centers.

We tracked our progress in the program, keeping audit reports for the data centers with follow-up documentation and statistics on corrective actions taken based on our recommendations.

In addition, we periodically briefed executive management of the data center operations and our reporting chain with summary charts showing progress and program metrics.

Under my management guidance, our team developed a smooth running operation.

Apart from our standard data center visits, at the request of one of the VPs in our commercial operation, I accompanied him and his staff to Quebec, Canada, to audit their data center. This was a fun trip.

The VP set us up to have the royal treatment, including first-class airline seats, accommodations at a five-star hotel, and limo service to the facility. It was my glimpse into how "the other half" lived.

After we got the program successfully off and running, I was also asked to lead an audit team of one of the computing division's subsidiaries in the Midwest. This audit included computing security, the subsidiary's financial and Human Resources (HR) scope, and salesforce operations.

As we proceeded to interview employees and review sales and financial stats, it became clear that the subsidiary was in trouble with finances and employees. Everyone agreed that the work environment was horrific. They said it was not only oppressive, but the level of combativeness and competition set up by the senior executives among most employees was debilitating. Good employees were bailing from the company.

The executives had consciously set up a dog-eat-dog, "me first" environment, thinking this was the best way to increase sales. It wasn't. A "we first" inclusive and respectful work environment could have garnered the results they were looking for.

At the end of the audit, as tough as my conclusion and recommendations were, and with the agreement of the entire audit team, I suggested firing the CEO, the COO, and the CFO and replacing them with team-oriented people.

As bold as my recommendations were, I sincerely felt that these critical moves were necessary to right the ship, and I did not hesitate to say so. My hope was that my recommendations would be acted on.

Somewhat to my relief, executive management overseeing this subsidiary accepted and acted quickly to replace the executive hierarchy in the subsidiary division.

The feedback I received was that my recommendations, having changed the environment, were applauded by the employees in the organization.

The home office hired new executives and clearly stated their expectations for improvement. We were informed that the new team would be tracked for results on how well things improved

Although I never heard any detailed results of what happened after our recommendations were implemented, I was aware that significant changes had been made by the new progressive, team-oriented management. Had things not worked out like this, I am sure I would have been contacted.

18

Tough Decision

Managing A Personnel Dilemma

In the work-a-day world, sometimes managers must handle awkward situations. These are especially critical when the situations involve employee issues. For me one unusual occurrence involved a key staff member of our team who refused to continue to do the work that he and the other members of our staff were routinely doing.

Over a couple of years, we had established a comprehensive and smooth-running computer security program. Most of the recommendations we made were implemented, and executive management was pleased with what we were doing and how we were doing it.

Our program became the model for the data centers in the services and commercial divisions.

I had stopped performing compliance audits myself, but the rest of the team continued to. As the organization manager, my focus continued to be program coordination with line and executive management, guiding our team and helping to resolve issues that came up in the course of audits.

Things were going well until this key staff member decided that continuing to perform the audits was beneath him. He and I had become good friends in the work environment, and I always appreciated his contributions and told him so. I thought everything was fine with him—that is, until the day he approached me and said, "I helped establish this program and have continued to be a primary focal point coordinating with our data center managers, but I don't feel that I should have to go out and perform audits anymore."

I was stunned and at first didn't know how to respond. He was a cornerstone of the program and did a fabulous job coordinating with the centers and performing audits. And he needed to continue doing the work as everyone else in our team was doing, including the audits.

I didn't react immediately but responded, "Let's discuss this in a few days. I need to consider what you have said."

I lost sleep over this issue for the next several days. On the one hand, I sincerely appreciated everything he contributed, and he was good with the data center managers. They all appreciated and enjoyed working with him.

On the other hand, as the manager of our team, I could not let him dictate what he did or didn't want to do. If I had, it would have created a rift with the others in the team. All of them were willing to do what was needed, including performing the audits. And if I had let him do what he wanted to, it would have undermined my leadership.

After thinking long and hard about the situation, I consulted our HR contact, a very supportive director I had known for a while. I sat with her and described the situation.

"I don't feel that I have any choice," I said regretfully, "but to tell him he needs to leave the organization. But I will say I will try to find him another job to his liking. I want to let him know how much I have appreciated him and all he has done, but that he has to leave if he is unwilling to do the job."

She considered this for a moment and responded, "I think you are on solid footing with this approach and it's great that you want to extend a hand to help him out when he leaves. That should send him a positive message about your feelings toward him."

The next day, he and I sat in my office and discussed the situation. I told him my decision and desire to help him find his next job. He looked at me and said nothing. Then he stood up and left.

I felt that I had offered him as much as I could out of personal and professional respect for him. Because of his disruptive attitude was to the rest of the team it was obvious to me that he could no longer be effective as part of our team.

Two days later, the HR director contacted me and handed me a letter this staff member had written accusing me of discrimination in the workplace. I was taken aback, and almost shocked that he would take this position. Needless to say, I was disappointed in him.

This was the only time in my career that someone lodged a complaint against me.

The HR director told me she saw no merit in his claim and would tell him so. She subsequently talked with him, advised him of her view, and gave him a letter detailing why his claim was without merit.

He returned to our area and announced that he would be leaving as soon as possible.

I said, "I would like to help you find another position. If you would update your resume to include your time with us, I will send it with a glowing recommendation to a number of my contacts in computing technology."

In a few days, he was offered a job with a commensurate salary in another company facility in our locale. He accepted it and left.

I did not feel good about this outcome. I hated to lose him and sever our relationship but felt it had worked out as well as could be expected. After he moved, he continued to stay in touch with our team administrative assistant, although he made no effort to communicate with me.

I really missed him and our previous great relationship. Shortly after he left, I wanted to reconnect with him and mentioned this to our administrative assistant. She told me that he was still bitter and didn't want to have any communication with me. I asked her to let me know if and when she thought it would be acceptable to him for me to reach out to him.

It took about ten months for him to feel comfortable contacting me. I called him, and we arranged to go out to lunch. He told me the new job was working well and that he appreciated my helping him get it. We caught up with each other on things going on with our team and in our personal lives.

As time passed, we stayed in touch and eventually mended our relationship and deepened it.

He shared many things with me—he was very happily married to a lovely lady who was an accomplished artist. It was obvious that he had always been passionately in love with her, and he doted on her.

She became deaf in her early twenties, but that did not affect their relationship or her work.

She passed away the year he retired. I don't know specifically what caused her death, but I recall it had something to do with a neurological condition that caused her deafness.

He was devastated. He had no other family, and after his wife's passing, he moved to Florida to the small town where he had grown up on the outskirts of the Everglades.

He once visited my wife and me and we had a great time. We agreed to stay connected and did for a while. Then suddenly, neither his email address nor his phone worked. I tried numerous times to contact him but never could. I got in touch with several people we both knew, but no one had any idea what had happened to him.

After all he and I had gone through—good and bad—ours was a relationship I cherished. At the end, we had rekindled our friendship and become good friends again. I was sorry when our contact ended, and he was a loss to me.

I have seen people in management and leadership positions purposely try to stay aloof in their relationships with subordinates to avoid emotional entanglements. They have unconsciously isolated themselves from their employees. Yes, I agree that relationships on the job need to remain professional, but aloofness doesn't work for me. I believe a good manager can maintain a professional demeanor while still showing personal appreciation and respect for employees as people.

19

Another Transition

With the advent of desktop and personal and laptop computers, the need for large data centers became obsolete, and our computing security program was phased out.

At the same time, the two VPs for whom I worked both retired, and our little team was disbanded. I went to work for two directors of computing in the technology division as an individual senior manager contributor without a staff or team. I was paired with a partner—another senior manager I had known who was a former director of ethics. We brought my former secretary on board and were given two small offices and an anteroom as our base of operation.

Our job was to interview and counsel employees in the tech division who were being laid off from the mainframe data centers because of the downsizing and eventual closure of these areas. We worked one-on-one with about eighty employees to help them plan their careers forward.

Technology had caught up with and surpassed the need for "big blue" computer centers. The lifelong jobs of people were vanishing who had supported and relied on large-scale computing for their livelihoods.

Most of these employees had no other skills or future employment and no place to go. And we were laying them off.

This was challenging work for me. I felt I could help these folks.

As I designed my approach, I realized that, first, we would have to address the shock and grief of losing jobs before anyone was ready to talk about where to go and what to do. Many of these employees had been in their positions for years.

When they came to see me it took some time to talk through their situations and reconcile where they were now.

We had to discuss their concerns, and, in some cases, anger, at being laid off after years of loyal service to the company.

Several sessions focused on why they were being laid off, candidly how they felt about it, and their comfort level with moving on.

In the first few sessions, much of my job in this stage of our discussions was simply to listen. Giving people an opportunity to vent and talk helped calm them and to start thinking about their next steps.

Of course, having been fired from my previous Security and Fire Protection position with no one to help me find another job, I could empathize with them, and counsel and assist them.

With each of them, I said, "I know this was none of your doing, and it was not a result of how well you did your job. It's just that the company no longer needs the function you are performing."

I made sure that I encouraged all of these people with the words that were never said to me in a similar situation, because I knew the hurt and anxiety they were feeling.

"This can be an opportunity for you to look ahead and consider what other avenues you can explore for employment, whether inside or outside the company. It could be the beginning of an exciting journey!"

I would ask each of them to jot down what skills they used to do their jobs, both technical skills related to tasks and, as important, the interpersonal skills they used with coworkers, their management, their customers, and associates.

Next, I would urge each person to ask themselves, "If you could do anything you wanted to do, what would that be?"

I said, "Don't limit yourself. Loosen up and dream! Don't worry about 'the how.' Write your ideas down. Be outrageous! Make a list that we can discuss together."

The follow-on sessions were exciting, and I was impressed at how openly folks jumped in and looked forward to future possibilities. This exercise allowed these employees to dream and explore without the burdens or paying attention to the negative questions: "But I'm not qualified," "I have no experience in this." "Who would hire me?"

As each person told me the kinds of things they would like to do, I wrote them down on my whiteboard, and we explored each idea in more detail.

Our discussions around all this created the groundwork for their forming a path forward.

I worked out the priorities for each of these folks. Did location for family and schools come first? Location because of a spouse's job? Driving miles to work? Salary? Type of business?

Then, assuming we were looking for a position in a relatively local company, we drew a circle on a map for the distance they were willing to travel and identified companies within that circle to research and consider.

These sessions were enlightening. As I worked closely with each of these employees, I got to appreciate their skill levels and their interests. Everything we discussed became more exciting and fun once they overcame the shock of losing their jobs. I thoroughly enjoyed getting to know each of them. And I was thrilled that I could help them. As we explored their options, when at first they were sure they had none, it was very gratifying to see their faces relax and even light up.

I must admit that helping to place some of these folks was difficult. Many had never had to look for a job before and needed to be more skilled in promoting themselves. We spent much time fashioning resumes and looking for places to circulate them.

My colleague and I were successful in helping about 85% of these folks find new jobs. I continued to coach some of them in their new positions.

Although highly unusual, one situation still stands out to me.

I worked with a lady in her late fifties who had been a tape librarian in one of our large-scale computing centers.

Her desire was to work for a Christian nonprofit, supporting people in foreign countries. She wanted to travel and become a member of a project team helping in a third-world country.

There was, and still is, a highly thought of, well-established, and prominent nonprofit headquartered in a nearby community doing this work. They are so well-run and successful that they rival the American Red Cross in responding to emergencies and disasters in other countries.

As it happened, I had a friend who knew the Information Technology Vice President (IT VP) for this company.

To make things even better, this company was also only a short drive from where this employee lived.

The IT VP took her under his wing, and they offered her a low-level job in the IT department. Once she accepted and joined them, I kept in touch with her. I told her she should make an effort to stand out by doing exemplary work and get to know the company's infrastructure and players in international project development and management.

It took about two more years before she applied for and was accepted to work on an international project as a project coordinator. She traveled with this project team to third-world countries and became an integral member of their operations. She was living her dream job.

I was ecstatic that she had found her way and was doing exactly what she wanted to do.

Please pass the potatoes.

20

Last Company Project

During the last years of my employment, I found myself in an unusual position. Essentially, I had worked myself out of a job, and yet I felt I still had more to contribute. I wasn't quite ready to retire and had an idea that might not only provide me with meaningful work but, more importantly, could be a genuine help to others.

In my years in management, as I have said in earlier chapters, I had learned firsthand that one's attitude and how one decides to treat people have everything to do with successful relationships, employee motivation and performance, and developing and sustaining a positive team environment for the best results. I knew that one's mindset on how to approach others is foundational.

In my last three years with the company, I was paired with another senior manager who was at the time also an individual contributor. He also had had years of management experience and had come to the same conclusions.

My partner had a good friend who was a Jesuit priest. At the time, this priest was an associate professor of ethics at a well-known Catholic university. He had a significant background studying and teaching ethics. We both felt that this priest could add value to any proposition we would consider.

The three of us put our heads together kicking around the idea for a workshop that could benefit employees and facilitate positive teaming in work groups—all based on attitude.

Much of the lecture material we subsequently developed was based on the priest's research into well-known philosophers and concepts about what makes people happy. Our challenge was to make this material applicable to the business environment.

We focused on the premise that increasing performance was linked to improving interpersonal relationships. We felt strongly that if we could engage participants to consider how they approached others, it could help facilitate a better work environment and help avoid and resolve conflict situations.

After we had come up with an outline and plan for a workshop, and what we saw as the benefits for attendees, I briefed the two directors for whom I worked on our idea. The directors immediately saw potential benefits for this project and approved of us going forward.

The workshop was free to participants and, since the supplies we needed came out of open company stores, there was no cost to us. Of course, my partner and I were employees on the company payroll, and the priest volunteered his time completely.

As we made clear, any employee could attend one of the workshops with the approval of their management, and the workshop was open to all employees on all shifts.

We were able to obtain a company course number through the internal education system so employees could get credit for attending the workshop.

It took us a couple of months to lay out the sessions, spicing up the lecture segments with interactive group discussions that supported and expanded on the lecture areas.

We found and reserved a company auditorium outside the secure company perimeter with ample free parking. Company credentials were not needed to get into the facility or to park. The auditorium held forty round tables of ten each.

We organized the day around lectures by the three of us, interspersed with guided tabletop discussions and experiential exercises among the participants.

In addition to laying out the workshop's daily agenda and co-facilitating the day's sessions, I was responsible for designing the workshop exercises and producing the visuals and handouts we used.

Very quickly, the workshop started a positive buzz in the company.

Shortly after starting the workshops, we received requests to attend from company line management and individual employees on all shifts. And we received requests from outside the company.

Calls came in from various businesses asking if their employees could attend our class, such as law firms asking if their board of directors could attend, migrant worker union leadership, tribal elders, nurses association leadership, and retail and nonprofit businesses. A typical table of ten included a mix of people from various organizations and both management and nonmanagement positions.

As people registered, we assigned those from the same organizations to different tables to get a variety of attendees at each table.

Our rule was that in introducing themselves at their tables, participants only used their first names and not identify their company or job or position descriptions or titles. Our aim was that participants interact as equals, not influenced by what they did, their job title or position, who they represented, or where they came from.

At the beginning of each workshop, to set the tone for the day, we asked the participants at their tables to answer the question, "Why am I here?"

Fully 90% answered the question by saying they were "here" to help others, to do something for others beyond themselves.

The three of us were astounded by this answer. Here we were in a business setting facilitating an all-day workshop among business people about attitude for cohesive organization teamwork, and immediately, people set the tone for the day of doing good beyond themselves! This response was consistent throughout all the workshops we held.

In the interactive table discussions, we focused on having participants "feel" for themselves the lessons of each subject enough to think about and absorb the premises we introduced.

Each of us facilitators wandered around the room among the tables to overhear the discussions at each table. As we listened, we were impressed with how candid people were about their concerns and likes and dislikes in the workplace, their appreciation or distrust of others in their groups, and other issues. These discussions were rich with good thinking and serious considerations.

Having recorded the table members' comments on flip charts after each exercise, table representatives gave their table read-outs of what group members took away from each exercise to the entire group. A total group discussion followed these read-outs.

We put on three workshops every month. At the beginning of each one, as people entered the auditorium, I could feel the surge of excitement. The positive energy was palpable. The word about the workshops had gotten around!

After every workshop, we asked every participant to complete a brief survey about the course, including their views of us as presenters, any suggestions for improvement, and what value the material was to them. Without exception, the comments were highly positive. Many noted that the material we taught would help them improve their work and personal relationships. This was tremendously inspiring and humbling to the three of us.

From the start of our workshops, I had always had a slightly uncomfortable feeling that what we were doing might not have the full backing at the highest level of management. I was therefore a little anxious when one day, midway through our first year of the training, I was unexpectedly summoned to the office of the Corporate Vice President of Human Resources. I knew who he was but had never met him.

I girded myself for the worst—to be reprimanded for not doing these workshops under his banner and without his executive approval—and with an order to stop. To my amazement, it was just the opposite, more positive than I could have ever imagined or hoped for!

As I entered his huge office, the VP rose from behind his desk, came toward me and introduced himself as we shook hands. We sat opposite each other on a small couch in his office.

He said, "Jed, I have heard from several people on my staff and elsewhere about the workshops you are conducting. I am so impressed that I wanted to ask you how I can help you and your team continue these."

His offer took me aback. I could hardly believe it. But boldly, I replied, "Well, sir, we could use some morning refreshments, maybe coffee, tea and muffins, box lunches with drinks, and a midafternoon snack and drinks. That would help us support the participants, but if that is too much . . .."

He interrupted me and said, "Consider it done. I will give you a contact to arrange all this. And the bill will come to my office."

Then he added," Do you need any more supplies or anything else I can help with?"

"No," I said. "What you have offered will be wonderful!"

I thanked him profusely and left.

I couldn't wait to return to our offices and tell the rest of our team.

They were ecstatic when they heard of his support and the supplies

he would contribute.

In my years of making presentations on various subjects, I have always felt that an important element is the wrap up. It is here, at the conclusion, that one has the opportunity to emphasize what one wishes the audience to take away and remember.

That said, at the conclusion of every workshop, I would read the following story entitled *"Are There Any Questions?"*

I don't recall where I found this, nor who the author is, but it was a fitting conclusion for our day's workshop.

In my subsequent work speaking at various events, I would always end with this story, and as I did, I would have someone hand out small quarter-size mirrors to the audience members.

> *Are There Any Questions?*
>
> *An offer that comes at the end of college lectures and long meetings is usually said when an audience is not only overdosed with information but when there is no time left anyhow. At times like that, you sure do have questions. Like "Can we leave now?" and "What the heck was this meeting for anyhow?" and "Where can I get a drink?"*
>
> *The offer is supposed to indicate openness on the part of the speaker, I suppose, but if, in fact, you do ask a question, both the speaker and the audience will give you drop-dead looks. And some fool—some earnest idiot—always asks.*
>
> *The speaker always answers by repeating most of what he has already said.*
>
> *But if there is a little time left and there is a little silence in response to the invitation, I usually ask the most important question of all: "What is the meaning of life?"*
>
> *You never know—somebody may have the answer, and I'd really hate to miss it because I was too socially inhibited to ask.*

But when I ask, it's usually taken as a kind of absurdist move—people laugh and nod and gather up their stuff, and the meeting is dismissed on that ridiculous note.

Once, and only once, I asked the question and got a serious answer. One that is with me still.

I went to an institute dedicated to human understanding and peace on the isle of Crete. At the last session on the last morning of a two-week seminar on Greek culture, led by intellectuals and experts in their fields, Alexander Papaderos rose from his chair at the back of the room and walked to the front, where he stood in the bright Greek sunlight of an open window and looked out.

We followed his gaze across the bay to the iron cross marking a German cemetery from World War II. He turned and made the ritual gesture: "Are there any questions?"

Quiet quilted the room. These two weeks had generated enough questions for a lifetime, but for now, there was only silence. "No questions?"

Papaderos swept the room with his eyes. So, I asked.

"Dr. Papaderos, what is the meaning of life?" The usual laughter followed, and people stirred to go. Papaderos held up his hand and stilled the room and looked at me for a long time, asking with his eyes if I was serious. He saw from my eyes that I was.

"I will answer your question." Taking his wallet out of his hip pocket, he fished into his leather billfold and brought out a very small round mirror about the size of a quarter. And what he said went like this:

"When I was a small child, during the war, we were very poor, and we lived in a remote village. One day, on the road, I found the broken pieces of a mirror. A German motorcycle had been wrecked in that place. I tried to find all the pieces and put them together, but it was not possible, so I kept only the largest piece. This one. And by scratching it on a stone, I made it round.

"I began to play with it as a toy and became fascinated by the fact that I could reflect light into dark places where the sun would never shine—in deep holes and crevices and dark closets. It became a game for me to get light into the most inaccessible places I could find.

"I kept the little mirror, and as I went about my growing up, I would take it out in idle moments and continue the challenge of the game.

"As I became a man, I grew to understand that this was not just a child's game but a metaphor for what I might do with my life.

"I came to understand that I am not the light or the source of the light. But light—truth, understanding, knowledge—is there, and it will only shine in many dark places if I reflect it.

"I am a fragment of a mirror whose whole design and shape I do not know. Nevertheless, with what I have, I can reflect light into the dark places of this world—into the black places in the hearts of men—and change some things in some people. Perhaps others may see and do likewise. This is what I am about. This is the meaning of my life."

And then he took his small mirror and, holding it carefully, caught the bright rays of daylight streaming through the window and reflected them onto my face and onto my hands folded on the desk.

Much of what I experienced in the way of information about Greek culture and history that summer is gone from memory.

But in the wallet of my mind, I carry a small round mirror still.

Are there any questions????

Reading this story always elicited quiet in the auditorium. After waiting for a moment, we ended each session by thanking everyone for attending and asking participants to think about the day's experience. And if there were takeaways they could use to improve their relationships, to please consider acting on what was relevant for them.

We concluded the workshops shortly before I retired. Over the three-year run, more than 10,000 people attended them. The project was a resounding success.

Please pass the potatoes.

21

Moving Forward

Shortly before I retired, my partner and I started our own part-time consulting company. Our aim was to assist organizations in developing and using a model for exceptional relationships. Some of the material reflected the principles we had discussed in the company workshops, with the addition of conflict resolution techniques, development of mission statements, and strategic and tactical plans to respond to the mission.

We named our company and incorporated it as The Institute for Personal and Professional Effectiveness (IPPE).

To ensure there was no conflict of interest with the workshops we conducted in the company, we sent our business proposal to our Corporate Ethics office and received their approval to start IPPE.

As IPPE, we focused on working with schools and small businesses to help establish forward-thinking strategies and responsive business plans and teach principles for exceptional relationships among staff and customers.

Our curriculum drew on basic concepts of ethics and integrity to convey the principles of personal and professional effectiveness. The curriculum included applying the principles of trust and respect to create and maintain dynamic organizations in which people wanted to freely contribute their full potential and goodwill.

My last in-company project was the workshop. After the three years of the workshops, my wife and I talked about my retirement. In my last year, when merit raises rolled around, the directors I worked for called me in to tell me that they sincerely appreciated all I was doing but that they could not offer me a raise or promotion.

I told them, "I appreciate everything you have done for me and I am fine with where I am financially. I have decided to retire in a few months, so everything is good."

I subsequently retired as planned without any fanfare. I packed up a small box of personal items, quietly said goodbye to a few folks, and left the building for the last time. As I did so, I recall feeling elated and that even with some hiccups along the way, I was satisfied with my career and what I had accomplished. I had no regrets and still don't.

My wife and I planned a small retirement party at the condo where we lived, and to my amazement, about sixty-five people showed up, one of whom was the president of one of the divisions I had supported.

I spent seventeen years climbing the ladder in Security and Fire Protection and a total of ten years in the computing division before I retired after twenty seven years with the company. My entire professional career spanned thirty-six years.

After I retired, I took a few months doing nothing, then launched in to building IPPE. I was able to garner several consulting contracts with schools and small businesses, but my heart wasn't in it.

The pressure of having to continue to market to attract business hung over me. My business partner was still employed full-time elsewhere and was not contributing to the business at all. Two years in, he and I decided very amicably to close down IPPE.

After IPPE, I incorporated my own business called JS Associates, essentially prepared to teach the same material in a different, more concise form. But my heart was not in that business either.

However, as I continued to refine the principles in an easy way for people to understand and use, I settled on a simple set of visuals and descriptors to convey the idea of managing one's attitude for exceptional relationships. These ideas are encapsulated in the two charts that follows: When I Choose "Me First" and When I Choose "We First".

In the past few years, I incorporated these into a book for adolescents called The Lion Who Flinched and have used them in speaking to audiences and workshops for youth and adults in various settings.

As I have used these charts and discussed them, I have noticed that people light up recognizing how being conscious of this material can help in their approaches to others.

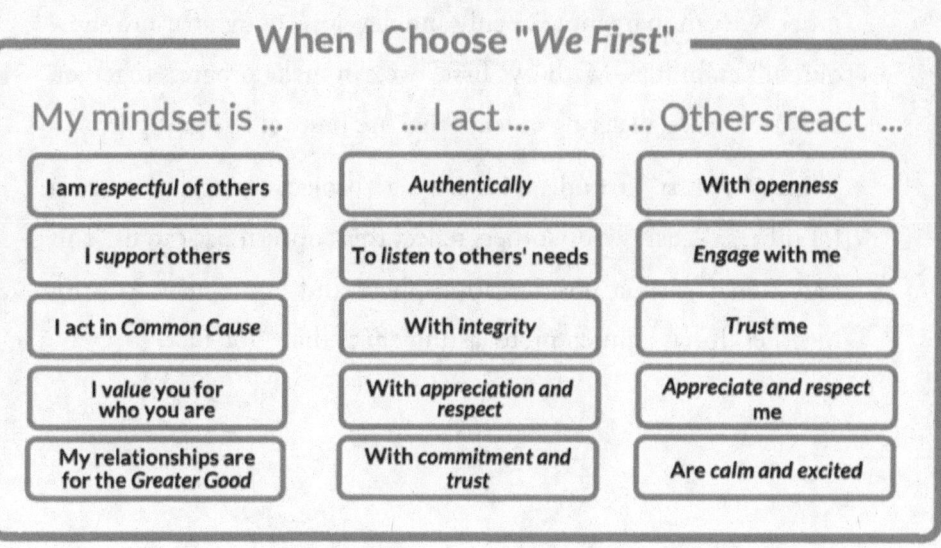

Takeaway

"We First" Instead of "Me First"

- To breed trust and respect, so we can do good things together, each of us must adopt a "we first" attitude.

- If any of us focuses on "me first," we will try to control and dominate each other. This emphasis will create distrust and prevent us from caring for and respecting each other. We will be unable to move forward and make progress together. We will not survive.

- "We first" is non-threatening. It is easier to be honest with each other. We can share more openly and develop enough trust to show our vulnerabilities. With "we first," we can make progress together, because we are all acting in ways that are best for the group.

- With a "we first" attitude, it is natural to project caring and concern for others. When we do, others reflect this concern back to us. This reflection creates a positive atmosphere and excitement to work together. It has a much more lasting effect than "me first."

Introspection

"Me First" or "We First"

The following exercise is to identify and work to improve a personal or professional relationship.

Think about an individual with whom you interact in which an element of anxiety and tension may be limiting your relationship.

- What is the basis of the anxiety and tension? Is it due to Me First attitudes and behavior? On whose part? Yours? The other person's? Both of you?

- How could you act differently to eliminate the anxiety and increase positive connections with that person? (Focus on We First attitudes and behavior.)

- In response to the above questions, what specific actions are you willing to take to improve this relationship?

- After taking these actions to improve this relationship, can you see changes in the reactions to your actions?

- What are they?

- Is the relationship improving?

- What additional actions can you take to continue to improve this relationship? Commit to taking these.

Expected Outcome: Developing a higher consciousness to manage oneself for exceptional relationships.

22

Beyond Business

All during my professional life in corporate America and since I retired, I have had a yearning do something for others beyond what I had done in my everyday jobs. This longing traces back to a critical time shortly after my father passed away, when I was a fifteen year-old and a sophomore in high school. At the time I was playing in a street pickup basketball game in our neighborhood and was paired with a kid my age, who I didn't know.

As we started, I yelled and passed him the ball, assuming he had heard me. Instead of turning around, he kept moving, and the ball hit him in the back of the head. He angrily turned to me and started mouthing sounds I could not understand. It was apparent that he was deaf.

Much of my family had been immersed in music for years, and it bothered me that this kid could not hear music.

I felt terrible about our meeting that way. I wanted to befriend him, but I did not want him to think I felt sorry for him because he couldn't hear.

(I had just gone through people feeling sorry for me about my Dad's dying, and as sincere as they were, I had enough of receiving sympathy.)

I needed to do something to relate to this boy. I decided to teach myself sign language to communicate with him on his terms. I went to the library and over a few weeks taught myself basic signing.

We became good friends. I had been babysitting for a couple of young sisters in our neighborhood and found out that their mother had been a speech therapist earlier in her life. I asked her if she felt qualified to work with my friend to teach him to read lips. She said she had those skills and would be happy to.

The three of us worked together for several months. In our sessions, I translated sign language for them to communicate as she taught him to read lips. In the process, I, too, picked up some capability to read lips. He and I stayed friends throughout the rest of my high school years, but then we lost touch.

Nevertheless, this experience kindled my desire to continue working with young people. Since then, I have gravitated toward situations where I can engage and support youth and families. This desire has taken me in several unusual directions.

While I was in college, I read to blind children. When I was in the Air Force, another Special Agent and I started a Boy Scout Troop in suburban Maryland, and we enlisted a friend of his to help.

We found a tobacco farmer in a nearby rural area who allowed us to set up a permanent campsite next to a manmade lake he stocked with fish.

We limited the Troop to thirty-five Scouts so we could pay enough attention to each of them individually. With the support of some of the Scouts' fathers, at least two of us leaders camped with the Troop every weekend, year-round.

I am a former ten-year member of both Kiwanis and Rotary Clubs, a ten-year disaster response manager for the American Red Cross and chair of our local chapter, and, for the past twenty-two years, the President, Executive Director and Co-Founder of a charitable all-volunteer nonprofit called "Caring Clowns International" (CCI). I have accepted that helping others is in my blood.

23

CARING CLOWNS INTERNATIONAL (CCI)

After my wife and I moved to the West Coast, and I joined the company, I wanted to continue to give back to the community in some volunteer capacity, preferably working to support kids and families. As I looked around for what to do, I found that the company had supported an all-volunteer clown club through its management association for years. It was (and still is) called the "Klown Klub," whose members perform at company and community events. I applied to become a clown.

Since I knew nothing about clowning, I was mentored by two experienced long-time clowns. I was a member of the Klub for most of my twenty-seven years with the company. We were all professional-grade quality clowns and entertained free wherever we were called to perform.

The "art of clowning" requires much information and involves many skills. It is more than just wearing a costume and a red nose. What I needed to master became very clear as I was mentored into the profession.

I learned the history and types of clowns, how to develop a clown persona and costume, how to design a face, and how to apply makeup. (There were times when I have been in makeup for eighteen hours in hot, humid weather, so knowing how to apply makeup is an important skill.)

Other necessary things to learn to round out my clowning capabilities were humorously exaggerated body movements, expressive facial gestures, talking patter with kids and adults, miming, and balloon art. The list goes on: close-up one-on-one magic, developing and performing clown skits and timing with other clowns, prop-making, and how to interact with children and adults with disabilities and children in hospitals. Some of our clowns were expert jugglers and unicycle riders, but me not so much. Clowning definitely is an art to be learned.

In 2000, a clown I didn't know invited me to accompany him with two other clowns to Vietnam. It was his second trip. His first trip was by himself as a novice clown, and it was overwhelming for him. He had just started clowning and found himself in a third-world country where clowns were unknown. He broke new ground by being there in makeup. Since I was retiring that year, I could not go. But I committed to and went with him and the other clown the following year, in 2001.

Back during my time on active military duty in the Pentagon, my security clearances prevented me from going to Vietnam since it was an active war zone. So, my first visit to the country was thirty-five years later, not as a military member but as a clown.

For me that first trip to Vietnam was a shocking and heart-wrenching experience I did not expect.

Many places we clowned were orphanages like dungeons overflowing with children abandoned by their families. Most of them had mental and physical disabilities or disfigurements.

In the Vietnamese culture, it was then, and may still be now, an embarrassment to have an other-than-normal child. And if a child was disabled in any way, most families did not have the financial capability to support the child. So, children—-some only weeks old—were left on the doorsteps of orphanages.

As I understood during that first trip, most of these children were maimed because of the chemicals we dropped in Vietnam during that war.

You've probably heard about Agent Orange, which the U.S. dropped along the North and South Vietnamese border to defoliate the jungles so South Vietnamese soldiers could see and prevent the North Vietnamese from getting to South Vietnam.

These poisonous chemicals leached into the ground and contaminated the groundwater used to cultivate gardens for food. The local population ate the vegetables from these gardens, not knowing the terrible havoc the chemicals would create long past the end of the war. As a result, pregnant mothers were giving birth to deformed babies.

If this isn't horrific enough, Agent Orange has a half-life of 500 years, so the problems continue.

I returned from that trip to Vietnam and told the other clowns I wanted to start an all-volunteer charitable nonprofit focusing on clowning and raising money to donate to other nonprofits supporting children and families in need.

I named our organization Caring Clowns International. Our mission statement reads:

> *"We clown to heal and expand the human spirit;*
> *people-to-people, country-to-country, and culture-to-culture.*
> *We fund projects which improve people's lives."*

A couple of clowns who went on my first trip to Vietnam with me have stayed with CCI for most of our twenty-two years. Through a two-weekend clown class I developed and several of us taught, we have attracted new members. The class is a short course on the elements and history of clowning. Our new members each get a mentor and learn as we do clown gigs.

Throughout our years, we have had clowns come and go. Today, we have about 15 members across the U.S. and in Vietnam, Peru, and Uganda.

We have clowned at events internationally and across the United States, in orphanages, children's and other hospitals, events for homeless children and adults, residences for abused women and children, schools for the disabled, retirement centers, VA hospitals, events for kids with down syndrome and disabilities, and children whose parents are in prisons and correctional facilities, community events and private parties.

We have performed for children and adults and provided funds to nonprofits helping children in Afghanistan, Angola, Bangladesh, Bolivia, Brazil, Canada, the Caribbean, the Dominican Republic, England, Ethiopia, France, Guatemala, Hong Kong, Italy, Kenya, Mexico, Nepal, Peru, Russia, Sierra Leone, South Africa, South Korea,

Thailand, Uganda, Ukraine, Vietnam, and throughout the United States.

Of particular note for me are the numerous trips we have made to Vietnam and Peru. In each of these countries, over the years, we have come to know many people.

For example, in Vietnam, on our first trip, I befriended a "cyclo" driver. (A cyclo is a pedal bike with a rear open seat bench for two or four passengers used like a taxi to transport tourists.) Although he did not speak English and I did not speak Vietnamese, we became good friends, miming to each other and laughing. Each time we visited I would see him. He was a small man, with big shining eyes. At our first sighting he would run full speed and jump into my arms like an excited little kid and embrace me kissing the side of my face, and I would hug him back tightly. We both always laughed at his greeting me this way. I loved it!

The second year, he and I sat in an outdoor market with our guide translating for us. He had a family of three children and a wife and was hoping to save enough to purchase a computer that his kids could learn to use. I quietly gave him money to purchase the computer. Each time we returned to Vietnam, I would seek out my cyclo driver, and we would enjoy each other for the brief time we were together.

We returned to Vietnam seven more times after our initial trip, clowning throughout the country. Our guide for our trips and I became good friends. He and I still communicate frequently, and, although it may never happen, I keep pushing him and his family to come visit my wife and me in the States.

We started visiting Peru after I was contacted by a plastic surgeon who had started an all-volunteer nonprofit called Komedyplast. The doctors perform free full facial surgeries for disadvantaged children. He asked if we in CCI would act as their entertainment element as they went to Lima, Peru, to the country's single public children's hospital. The surgeries are complicated eight-to-nine-hour procedures.

The jobs we clowns perform are to play with the kids and their families waiting to be evaluated by the doctors on "Screening Day," the first Saturday of the trip, so the doctors can determine which children are to be operated on.

From early in the morning on Screening Day, up to three hundred families from all over Peru line up waiting to see the doctors in the hope their children will be operated on. Some families travel two or three days by bus from as far away as the Amazon basin.

The doctors perform an average of twenty surgeries during the ten-day mission, so most families and their children who show up for consideration are not selected. The last hour of Screening Day is always tense, as most families are told their children will not be receiving surgery.

Once the doctors provide me with the schedule for the week's surgeries, I have the list of which children will be getting surgery, when, and the time they are scheduled to be in post-op recovery. We clowns are with each child and their family just before the children are given anesthesia and wheeled into the operating room. So, we are the last people the kids see before surgery. When they are in post-op and lucid, we show up again to brighten them up, play with them, and give each of them a stuffed animal.

The doctors always comment on how quickly the children recover, having had us there with them before and after their surgery.

Between surgeries, we clown in the hospital courtyard for about four hundred kids each day, and then on each ward and an adjacent free clinic, doing balloon animal sculptures and handing out toys and stuffed animals to bedridden children. And we always clown around with hospital staff!

Our fifteenth year traveling with Komedyplast was in 2020 when we clowned for children in the 300-bed hospital. As in Vietnam, we have developed close "family" ties with the Peruvian people and with the team of doctors. Because of COVID, we have not yet returned to Peru to support these surgical missions.

From the earliest trips to Peru, many children return year after year to say hello to the doctors and the clowns. After fifteen years, these "children," who were ages five to seven when they had surgery, come back repeatedly. They grew into beautiful young adults. Although we clowns do not know most of their names, they and their families became our families, and every year they come back is a celebration of love.

Employing our grant process, we continue to financially support more than sixty-five well-established nonprofits in developing countries and the United States. As of this writing, we have donated $542,000 to other nonprofits.

Our members and donors recommend nonprofits for us to support. After I research and vet potential recipient organizations, our Board Grant Committee reviews the completed grant application we require. The committee makes a recommendation to our Board on which organizations to fund and for how much. The Board makes the final decision. Our grants average $3,000-$5,000, although we have given $10,000 to some organizations, typically for disaster relief programs.

Since we are an all-volunteer nonprofit with no tangible assets, we maintain an overhead cost of about 7%, so most of the funds donated to us go to other nonprofits supporting children and families in need. (Most well-run nonprofits in the U.S. have an average of 35% overhead because they hire employees, own vehicles, and property, pay for services, etc. We, of course, do not.)

The funds we raise to donate to other nonprofits come from a small loyal base of people who contribute annually to CCI. In the past, we have also put on dinner auctions to raise funds. These were always fun and unique as dinner auctions go because we clowns always dressed for the occasions and, for entertainment, put on several original clown skits. However, the work involved in organizing and managing these events became overwhelming for the few of us involved, given the amount of funds raised.

Several months before and after the events, four or five of us would spend 40-50 hours a week planning for these events and doing the post-event accounting and correspondence.

Since our last dinner auction, we have gone to online fundraisers, advertising to our donor base a "non-auction" and suggesting that instead of taking the time and effort to attend a fundraising event, they donate directly to CCI. Surprisingly, we have raised the same amount of money without the time and cost to put on an in-person dinner auction.

Throughout our travels, we have reached hundreds of thousands of children and adults through the joy of clowning. Their responses in receiving the balloon sculptures, red noses, and stuffed animals we have passed out are uplifting for everyone and all the "thank you's" humbling for us clowns.

This year, in 2024, we are celebrating our 22nd anniversary.

You may learn more about Caring Clowns International at www.caringclownsinternational.org.

24

Conclusion

My varied experiences, many of which I have shared here, have led me to several conclusions.

As trite as it may sound, I think that humbly looking to do good beyond ourselves is foundational to enjoying life. I know from my own experience that understanding and embodying the elements of "We First" is key.

Giving beyond ourselves can help us to not prejudge but to approach others with an open mind, increasing the capability for exceptional collaborations and results and positive, long-lasting relationships.

I believe that we each can manage much of what happens to us by how we manage ourselves and our attitudes.

For the most part, we can decide how to act and react as we face different situations and develop relationships with others.

As of this writing, I continue to manage and be an active clown in CCI. But I am always on the lookout for other opportunities to contribute.

I wrote this free verse at the conclusion of my first trip clowning to Vietnam. It is an appropriate final word here.

If you have ever thought about giving—in any manner, in any degree, for any cause or people you feel are worthwhile, do it.

Do it now.

It is the definition of Life itself.

It creates infectious joy and love. It breeds "caring for" at its foundation.

Be part of the Universe.

Give yourself away to others.

You will reap unbelievable riches from not wanting them.

Please pass the potatoes.

Mastering Oneself for Exceptional Relationships

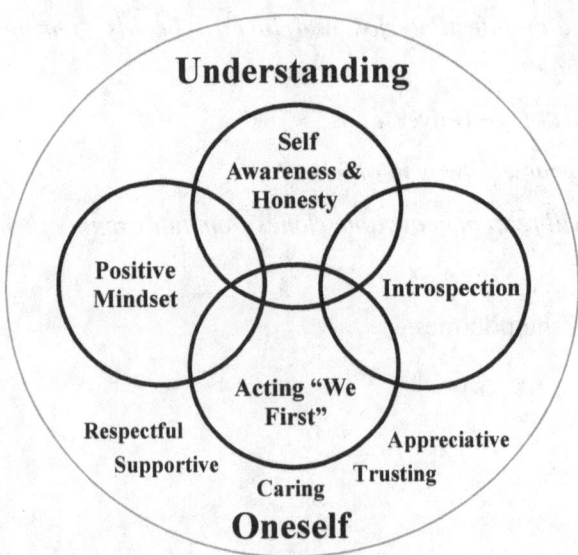

The only thing we can control is our own attitude.
How I get along with you is up to me not you.

These principles apply to everyone in any situation.

The essential tools for self-management and successful relationships
are in two companion books.

- *"The Lion Who Flinched"* is a parable focused for adolescents and adults who work with youth.
- *"Please Pass the Potatoes"* expresses these tools in a memoir for adults in business.

Both books are available from booksellers at *www.jedselter.com*.

Contact Jed for information on workshops though his website.

Copyright © 2024 Jed Selter

A companion book entitled The *Lion Who Flinched* discusses many essential tools for self-management and successful relationships expressed in *Please Pass the Potatoes*.

The Lion book is a parable about a young lion cub who learns how to manage himself to have good relationships. This book focuses on students and is being used in K-12 classrooms and graduate college levels.

More About the Author

Jed's heartfelt passion for people and his perspectives on relationships began when he was a teenager.

Throughout his career, he has been a keynote speaker at forums on the topics of motivation, leadership, and effective management.

Also on a volunteer basis, he has mentored and continues to mentor many people for better career opportunities and exceptional relationships.

Jed holds a BS degree in Sociology/Psychology from Iowa State University. He is a graduate of several Air Force and industry executive management programs.

"Please Pass the Potatoes" is Jed's fourth published book.

You may order this and Jed's other books from your favorite bookstore or online bookseller:

The Lion Who Flinched

The Journey

Behind the Grease Paint—A Clown's Chronicle in Vietnam

You may contact Jed and find more information about him and his work at *www.jedselter.com*.

www.ingramcontent.com/pod-product-compliance
Lightning Source LLC
LaVergne TN
LVHW032012070526
838202LV00059B/6413